# TEACHER'S MANUAL

SECOND EDITION

# THE BASICS OF SPEECH

*learning to be a
competent communicator*

## GALVIN ■ COOPER ■ GORDON

National Textbook Company
a division of *NTC Publishing Group* • Lincolnwood, Illinois USA

# CONTENTS

### UNIT I  PROGRAM HIGHLIGHTS                                          1

The Philosophy of *The Basics of Speech*                                1
Organization of the Text                                                3
Organization of the *Teacher's Manual*                                  5
Adapting to Varying Ability Levels                                      6
Cultural Diversity and Students with Special Needs                      7
Course Management                                                      14
Assessment                                                             16
Notes                                                                  21

### UNIT II  TEACHING SUGGESTIONS                                      23

**PART ONE  THE BASICS OF COMMUNICATION**                             23

*Chapter 1*  The Communication Process                                 24
*Chapter 2*  Elements of Communication                                 30
*Chapter 3*  The Work of Speaking and Listening                        39
*Chapter 4*  The Competent Communicator                                58

**PART TWO  COMMUNICATION WITH SELF AND OTHERS**                      85

*Chapter 5*  Communication and Your Self                               85
*Chapter 6*  Communication with Others                                 94

**PART THREE  GROUP COMMUNICATION**                                  108

*Chapter 7*  Communication in Groups                                  109
*Chapter 8*  Forms of Group Discussion                                123

**PART FOUR  PUBLIC COMMUNICATION**                                  133

*Chapter 9*   Introduction to Public Speaking                         134
*Chapter 10*  Finding and Using Information                            141
*Chapter 11*  Constructing the Speech                                 155
*Chapter 12*  Delivering the Speech                                   164
*Chapter 13*  Creating the Informative Speech                         173
*Chapter 14*  Creating the Persuasive Speech                          181
*Chapter 15*  Learning About Debate                                   189

**PART FIVE  INTERPRETIVE COMMUNICATION**                            195

*Chapter 16*  Preparing for Oral Interpretation                       196
*Chapter 17*  Performing Oral Interpretation                          201
*Chapter 18*  Group Interpretation                                    213

### UNIT III  RESOURCES                                               223

Resources for Professional Growth                                     223
Part Resources                                                        228

### UNIT IV  BLACKLINE MASTERS                                        235

*Section A*  Worksheets and Evaluation Forms                          236
*Section B*  Handouts                                                 296
*Section C*  Chapter Tests and Answer Key                             306

# PROGRAM HIGHLIGHTS

## The Philosophy of *The Basics of Speech*

Understanding and expressing ideas effectively are important skills that students need to acquire. Yet, too often, these essential communication skills are ignored by educators who assume that, because children begin school already talking, they need no direct instruction in listening and speaking. Nothing could be further from the truth, particularly when children reach adolescence.

Young adolescents are concerned about building relationships with their peers, becoming more adept at socializing, formulating reasons for their actions and beliefs, evaluating the messages of others, and becoming more skilled at speaking in front of others. They experiment with different behaviors and interpret others' reactions to these behaviors. They are attempting to answer the questions "Who am I?" and "How do I fit in?"

Young adolescents are beginning to work on developmental tasks that will move them toward adulthood. Barbara Wood[1] identifies competent adolescents as those who do the following:

1. Gain and maintain the attention of others in socially acceptable ways.

2. Use others as resources when a task is difficult.

3. Express both affection and hostility to others.

4. Assume control in peer-related activities or follow the lead of others (for example, give suggestions and follow suggestions).

5. Express both affection and hostility to peers.

6. Compete with peers—exhibit interpersonal competition.

7. Praise themselves or show pride in their accomplishments.

8. Give evidence of opinion to support a plan of action.

9. Present a variety of arguments to support a plan of action.

10. Take into account another person's point of view in talking with that person, especially if asked to do so.

11. Present and understand information in messages related to objects and processes not immediately visible.

12. Read effectively the feedback of others to a message; supply relevant feedback to others when they communicate.

13. Evaluate the messages of others critically and make appropriate comments regarding such evaluations.

14. Take the role of another person effectively without being pushed to do so.

15. Construct contrary-to-fact propositions.

16. Present a conceptualization of their own thoughts, as well as the thoughts of others.

17. Give, as well as understand, complex referential messages; adapt referential messages to the needs of others.

It is the goal of this text to help students become confident in their abilities to communicate. The educational experiences are chosen to help them decide who they are and how they fit in. Therefore, the text is based on the five communication functions identified by Wood in her description of a Speech Communication Association study.

1. *Controlling.* These are communication acts in which the participants' dominant function is to control behavior: for example, commanding, offering, suggesting, permitting, threatening, warning, prohibiting, contracting, refusing, bargaining, rejecting, acknowledging, justifying, persuading, and arguing.

2. *Feeling.* These are communication acts that express and respond to feelings and attitudes, such as exclaiming, expressing a state or an attitude, taunting, commiserating, tale telling, blaming, disagreeing, and rejecting.

3. *Informing*. These are communication acts in which the participants' function is to offer or seek information: for example, stating information, questioning, answering, justifying, naming, pointing out an object, demonstrating, explaining, and acknowledging.

4. *Ritualizing*. These are communication acts that serve primarily to maintain social relationships and to facilitate social interaction, such as greeting, taking leave, participating in verbal games, reciting, taking turns in conversations, participating in culturally appropriate speech modes (for example, teasing, shocking, punning, praying), and demonstrating culturally appropriate amenities.

5. *Imagining*. These are communication acts that cast the participants in imaginary situations and include creative behaviors such as role-playing, fantasizing, speculating, dramatizing, theorizing, and storytelling.

## Organization of the Text

Because oral communication is a skill that is learned by doing, the text stresses an activity approach. *The Basics of Speech* uses an active, conversational style to present basic concepts. Students are then asked to apply the concepts to important areas of their lives by observing the people around them, interacting with those people, and recording their ideas and feelings.

The text consists of five parts. Part One begins with Chapter 1, which defines *communication* and presents an overview of the communication process. Chapters 2, 3, and 4 focus on the elements of communication—voice production, the listening process, and the competent communicator. Part Two consists of two chapters. Chapter 5 focuses on self-concept as it relates to communication. The role of communication in the development of interpersonal relations is discussed in Chapter 6. Part Three emphasizes small-group communication. The nature of groups, forms of small-group discussion, and problem-solving groups are discussed in Chapters 7 and 8. Formal groups such as symposiums, panel discussions, and round tables are highlighted. Parliamentary procedure is introduced. Part Four focuses on public speaking, emphasizing informative speeches and social ritual speeches. Chapters 9–13 examine the skills of selecting a topic, analyzing an audience, researching a topic, organizing a speech, and delivering a speech. Chapters 14 and 15 investigate persuasive speeches and classroom debate. Oral interpretation is covered in Part Five. The three final chapters (16–18) discuss the steps in preparing oral interpretation. Choral speaking, reader's theatre, and storytelling are also discussed.

Each chapter contains the following elements:

1. *Objectives*—Specific learning goals set at the beginning of each chapter.

2. *Key Words*—List of important words that are introduced in the chapter.

3. *Observe*—Assignments designed to help students develop analytic skills. The activities require students to see and hear what is going on around them so they can respond in the most effective way.

4. *Interact*—Activities involving communication between at least two people. They require students to listen, evaluate a message, and respond.

5. *Apply*—Sections of the text that offer students an opportunity to pause and think about the reading and perhaps to apply it to their own frame of reference.

6. *Journal Entries*—Actual diary entries written by teenagers about the chapter topic.

Each chapter ends with a section entitled "Summary." This section includes:

1. *Think About It*—Chapter review questions that reinforce material discussed in the chapter.

2. *Try It Out*—Oral communication activities that apply the concepts discussed in the chapter.

3. *Put It In Writing*—Assignments that ask students to record their ideas in a journal, to analyze an event they have observed, or to describe what might happen in the future.

4. *Speak About It*—Communication activities that require students to speak in front of the class or in front of a small group about concepts discussed in the chapter. This section also enables students to gradually build public speaking confidence.

## OBSERVE, INTERACT, AND APPLY

Included within each chapter of the text are special assignments that ask students to *observe* the communication behaviors around them, *interact* with fellow students, or *apply* the communication concepts presented in the text. For example:

Observe two classmates having a typical conversation in the cafeteria. Pay careful attention to the behavior of each person when he or she is not speaking. Record the ways each person stays active in the conversation while listening.

With a partner, take turns recalling a past experience when each of you, a family member, or a friend assumed what the other was thinking and this caused a misunderstanding. Discuss how the problem could have been avoided.

Communication is part of almost every job. From the following list of career opportunities, try to select one in which communication skills would *not* be a basic job requirement. Explain your choice.

As the examples indicate, the Observe activities stress critical thinking and observation skills; the Interact activities require students to practice their communication skills in pairs or small groups; and the Apply activities require students to test their knowledge and predict outcomes. All of these experiences are essential, since competent communicators must be able to observe, analyze, and predict, in addition to developing speaking and listening skills.

The Observe, Interact, and Apply activities can be used in a variety of ways:

1. To stimulate class discussions

2. For journal assignments

3. For student reports

4. For role-play activities

5. To create class projects

6. In combination with activities included in this *Teacher's Manual.*

# Organization of the *Teacher's Manual*

The goals of the student text are to increase students' self-understanding through communication and to improve students' communication skills in a variety of contexts. The activities in the *Teacher's Manual* support and extend these goals.

Unit I presents general information necessary to effectively prepare for the course.

Unit II provides Part highlights and chapter-by-chapter teaching suggestions. For each chapter there are overviews, chapter objectives, and a wide variety of Warm-Up and Critical Thinking activities. The Critical Thinking activities provide opportunities for developing a broad range of competencies in a variety of contexts. Each activity is identified as appropriate for

 individual work,

work in pairs,

or work in small groups or as a class.

Critical Thinking activities are structured into objectives, materials needed, procedures, follow-up activities, assessment procedures, and enrichment. A ❑ designates reproducible handouts, evaluation forms, and worksheets, which are included in Unit IV of the *Resource Book*.

Unit III is an in-depth bibliography of additional resources for teachers. The first section contains resources for professional growth, including books and articles, lists of professional associations, and addresses of companies that offer teaching aids. The second section contains both print and nonprint resources for each Part of *The Basics of Speech*.

# Adapting to Varying Ability Levels

## ADJUSTING INSTRUCTION

This *Teacher's Manual* includes many activities for each chapter, so that you can pick and choose those most relevant to the ability levels of the students in your classes. Some activities will be more appropriate for students who are having difficulty in communicating effectively; others will be more appropriate for advanced students.

Each activity in this *Teacher's Manual* includes an enrichment activity. This may be used to help students further their skill development—particularly those students who are somewhat advanced in their communication ability.

All activities in this *Teacher's Manual* (as well as Interact, Observe, and Apply activities in the text) can be adapted. For example, in an activity requiring students to interview five people, students who are having difficulty communicating may interview only two people. The following two guidelines might be of help.

1. Students having difficulty with the concepts in the text may respond well to individualized contact with a teacher. Thus, you may want to schedule individual conferences to discuss a student's written work or in-class performance. On a daily basis, providing a word of encouragement or asking students questions they can answer will also help to encourage less able students.

2. It is probably wise to schedule the performances of less able students near the end of the performance schedule. This allows them more time to prepare. It also provides them with possible models and the benefit of hearing critiques of other performances.

Some students, regardless of ability, may be apprehensive about communicating. Research suggests that as many as 20 percent of the students in any school exhibit high levels of communication apprehension.[2] The following suggestions are effective ways to reduce this apprehension:

1. Give these students more individualized instruction and encouragement.

2. Establish good rapport with and among students (see section on classroom climate on page 15).

3. Reinforce students' positive oral responses and communication with others.

4. Utilize one-to-one and small-group activities.

## TEACH-RETEACH OPTIONS

Sometimes students do not grasp concepts on their first exposure. Developing skills such as speaking and listening often requires many practice sessions. We have included activities for both teaching and reteaching. You might use one activity to teach and the enrichment section of the activity to reteach.

Teach-reteach options can be increased by using the Interact or Observe activities in the text in conjunction with the activities in this *Teacher's Manual.* You might use an Interact or Observe activity to teach a concept or skill and then use an appropriate activity from this *Teacher's Manual* as a reteach option. For example, you could use the first Interact in Chapter 2 (page 22) to teach students that the same word can have different meanings. Then you could reteach the concept by using the "Oh, You Meant . . ." activity in the *Teacher's Manual.* Alternatively, the *Teacher's Manual* activity could be used to teach and the text activity to reteach. The end-of-chapter activities could be used in conjunction with the *Teacher's Manual* activities in the same way.

# Cultural Diversity and Students with Special Needs

Although the entire *Teacher's Manual* considers students' ability levels, this section focuses specifically on students from culturally diverse backgrounds, gifted and talented students, mainstreamed students, and students at risk. Several concerns for teaching these groups are included in this section, as well as activities specifically appropriate for these groups.[3]

## CULTURAL DIVERSITY

There is wide diversity of cultural background in today's classrooms. Yet, as J. Condon argues, the classroom culture is, to a great extent, an extension of mainstream American culture.[4] For example, the values of the classroom are those of mainstream America—independence, competition, individualism, and concern for relevance and application. As a culture, such as African-Americans, Hispanics, Southeast Asian refugees, Native Americans, and other ethnic minorities, may have a difficult time adjusting to the classroom culture.

This is true because culture influences both behavior and psychological processes. It affects the way we perceive the world. Culture "forms a prism through which members of a group see the world and create 'shared' meanings."[5]

This creating of shared meanings can be frustrating and fraught with misunderstanding! One way to improve communication is to be sensitive to the stumbling blocks to intercultural communication. These stumbling blocks have been defined as:

1. *Assuming similarity instead of difference.* There seem to be no universals of human nature that can be used as a basis for automatic understanding. Each of us is so unconsciously influenced by our own culture that we assume the basic needs, desires, and beliefs of others are the same as our own.

2. *Language.* Even "yes" and "no" can cause trouble. When a Japanese person hears, "Won't you have some tea?" she listens to the literal meaning of the sentence and answers, "No," meaning she wants some.

3. *Nonverbal misinterpretations.* When we enter into another culture, we need to be able to hear its "special hum and buzz of implication." When we do not comprehend or when we misinterpret the nonverbal cues, communication will be ineffective.

4. *Preconceptions and stereotypes.* These reduce the chance for effective communication because they interfere with our ability to objectively view a situation.

5. *Tendency to evaluate.* When we approve or disapprove the actions or statements of another, rather than try to comprehend, effective communication is difficult. We need to remain open-minded. Otherwise, communication may be cut off before we really understand the other person.[6]

The cultural differences of our students are important to understand for two major reasons: (1) cultural differences may result in differences in learning style; and (2) understanding cultural differences can help us communicate more effectively with our students.

In the past decade, considerable research has focused on students' learning styles. Students appear to have preferences for the ways in which they process information (for example, concretely or abstractly) as well as the ways in which they receive information (for example, aurally or visually). Research supports the general conclusions that some Hispanic-American, Native American, African-American, and female students respond better to teaching methods that emphasize holistic and cooperative learning approaches, valuing of personal knowledge, concrete orientation, the oral tradition, and a reliance on imagery and expressiveness.

This learning style may be quite different from that of "traditional" students, whose learning style is characterized by abstract, independent, written, or technical orientation.

Remember that although general statements such as these can be made as a result of this research, careful attention must be given to individual differences so that stereotyping can be avoided.

Understanding cultural differences can help us communicate more effectively. For example, some African-American children use vocal response that is meant to reinforce the speaker ("yeah," "go on," "right on"). Often Anglo-American teachers view this interaction as an interruption rather than a reinforcement. Looking at the teacher is a sign of disrespect in certain Jamaican and African cultures, but a sign of respect in most U.S. cultures. This difference in nonverbal appropriateness could cause misunderstanding unless the teacher is aware of such differences.

To help you prepare to teach a diverse group, we would suggest the following:

1. Understand nontraditional learning styles and adapt lessons to them whenever possible.

2. Learn about the history and culture of nontraditional groups.

3. Research the contributions of women and ethnic minorities.

4. Uncover your own biases.

5. Learn about bias in instructional materials.

6. Learn about your school's resources for nontraditional students.

Finally, use a variety of teaching methods. Provide opportunities for students to work cooperatively as well as individually. Supplement lectures with audiovisual materials, discussions, simulations, role-plays, and active, hands-on experiences. Give students choices in how to complete an assignment—for example, a paper, an art project, or an oral report. Allow them to speak about aspects of their own cultures.

## STUDENTS WITH SPECIAL NEEDS

You know that you will find all types of students in your classroom. With mainstreaming mandated by federal law (Public Law 94-142), some of your students may have learning disabilities. Space does not allow an in-depth discussion of students with special needs; however, books have been written on each of the following categories of students, and several references for further reading are at the end of this section.

### THE LEARNING-DISABLED STUDENT

Learning-disabled students often have low self-concepts and often are less accepted and more overtly rejected than their peers without learning disabilities. They frequently have problems interacting with teachers and parents and exhibit problem behaviors in general. Many students with learning disabilities have negative verbal interaction and misinterpret nonverbal communication. Furthermore, in adolescence, some learning-disabled students are at risk for juvenile delinquency.

Students with learning disabilities usually demonstrate a discrepancy between their actual level of performance and their intellectual potential. These students have difficulty processing aural and visual stimuli, resulting in faulty interpretive responses.

Generally, learning-disabled students need a structured classroom environment. Following are general guidelines for working with learning-disabled students:[7]

1. Increase attention span by removing distractions, including any materials other than those necessary for the assigned task.

2. Try to improve one behavior at a time, rewarding appropriate behavior, and involving the student in recording behavioral progress. Discuss appropriate ways to expend extra energy.

3. Carefully structure the learning environment and tasks with specific standards, limits, and rules.

4. Consistency is an important ingredient in rules, directions, and the like. Make consequences for rule infractions clear.

5. Assign one task at a time, using a step-by-step procedure. This means short, sequential assignments with breaks between tasks.

6. Use a variety of media to present content (films, tapes, printed material).

7. Utilize active methods (simulation games, experiments, role-playing) in the instructional strategies.

8. Employ materials for differing learning styles (pictures, tapes, concrete objects).

## THE INTELLECTUALLY GIFTED STUDENT

Intellectually gifted students often progress academically as much as one and a quarter years within one calendar year. Usually gifted students possess some of the following characteristics: an interest in books and large reading vocabularies, ability to express themselves verbally in a mature way, a wide range of interests, a high level of abstract thinking, and a curiosity about learning.

Instructional materials and programs for the gifted abound. In general, the following instructional procedures often prove helpful:

1. Develop units of work that provide opportunity for in-depth and long-term activities, as well as library research. For example, students might write a TV script for a documentary, set up and conduct the interviews, make and edit a videotape, and present the finished product to the class.

2. Utilize special tables and bulletin boards for interesting and challenging problems, puzzles, and worksheets. Often gifted students will finish an assignment earlier than other students. A table with additional activities related to the content being studied can provide opportunities for students to expand their knowledge.

3. Use special enrichment materials appropriate to the content areas—films, videos, guest speakers, and field trips are a few examples.

4. Encourage oral and written reports on topics under discussion and related topics—debates, group discussions, role plays, and other active strategies are very effective for gifted students.

5. Challenge creative thinking by using games and simulation. Students might even create some of their own to share with classmates.

6. Encourage gifted students to participate in extracurricular speech activities.

## THE MAINSTREAMED STUDENT

Mainstreaming is the practice of integrating students who had previously been enrolled in special education classes into the regular classroom.

Regardless of the nature of the student's disability, the following general guidelines should be helpful:

1. Build rapport with the student. Let mainstreamed students know you are genuinely interested in seeing that they overcome their difficulties. A comfortable, relaxed atmosphere enhances rapport.

2. Adjust the length of the instructional session to fit the student's attention span. In fairly long sessions, you will need frequent changes of activities. Repeated drill may be necessary because of slower retention.

3. The mainstreamed students' interests need to be utilized. When students are interested in particular topics (a hobby, game, sport, or the like), they should be able to use these interests as speech topics.

4. Present each new concept by using several teaching techniques, such as questioning, role-playing, discussion, and demonstration. Reinforcing the same idea in various ways is extremely helpful to many mainstreamed students.

5. Pair mainstreamed students with other students for coaching and rehearsal of oral performances.

## AT-RISK STUDENTS

In a very real sense, all of the groups discussed previously are at risk. However, for our purposes, the at-risk student is defined as "one who is in danger of failing to complete his or her education with an adequate level of skills."[8] At-risk students may be characterized by any of the following academic difficulties: high absenteeism, lack of motivation, inattentiveness, distractibility, narrow range of interest, discipline problems, low self-esteem, short attention span, fear of failure, and lack of social skills.

When teaching at-risk students, the following suggestions may prove helpful:

1. Create a supportive classroom environment so students feel comfortable and accepted.

2. Use a wide range and variety of materials.

3. Set realistic goals and objectives for students and communicate these to them.

4. Be firm, consistent, and fair in classroom management.

5. Provide immediate feedback to student responses.

6. Actively engage students in the learning process. Providing a choice of ways to complete an assignment is especially helpful with at-risk students.

7. Use cooperative learning groups in which students are given a specific task and must work together to perform it. The essence of cooperative learning is assigning a group goal (preparing an advertisement for a product, performing a group skit) and rewarding the entire group on the basis of the quality of the finished product.

8. Avoid lecturing whenever possible.

## SUGGESTIONS FOR FURTHER READING

Burstein, N. D., and B. Callello. "Preparing Teachers to Work with Culturally Diverse Students: A Teacher Education Model." *Journal of Teacher Education* (Sept.–Oct. 1989): 9.

"Dealing with Diversity: At-Risk Students." Special issue of *Educational Leadership* 46. (Feb. 1989).

Frymier, J., and B. Gansneder. "The Phi Delta Kappa Study of Students At-Risk." *Phi Delta Kappan* (Oct. 1989): 142–145.

Gannon, S. R., and R. A. Thompson. "Cross-Culturalism in Children's Literature: Proceedings and Selected Papers from the 1987 International Conference of the Children's Literature Association." New York: Pace University, 1987.

Grant, C. A. "The Persistent Significance of Race in Schooling." *The Elementary School Journal* 88 (5) (1988): 561–572.

Haberman, M. "Preparing Teachers for Urban Schools." *Fastback* 267. Bloomington, IN: Phi Delta Kappa, 1989.

Heslep, R. D. "Education in PL94–142." *Journal of Research and Development in Education* 22 (4) (Summer 1989): 1–13.

Johnson, D., and F. Johnson. *Joining Together.* 3rd ed. Englewood Cliffs, NJ: Prentice-Hall, 1987.

Johnson, S., and V. Johnson. *Motivating Minority Students.* Springfield, IL: Charles C. Thomas, 1988.

Keller, C. *Learning Disabilities.* Washington, DC: National Education Association, 1987.

Kochman, T. "Black Style in Communication." In *Intercultural Communication: A Reader.* 5th ed. Edited by L. A. Samovar and R. E. Porter. Belmont, CA: Wadsworth, 1988. 130–138.

Levin, H., and K. Mann. "The Nature and Functions of Teacher Talk in a Classroom for Mentally Retarded Learners." *The Elementary School Journal* 86 (Nov. 1985): 185–198.

Mannix, D. *Oral Language Activities for Special Children.* West Nyack, NY: Center for Applied Research in Communication, 1990.

Margolis, H., and E. Schwartz. "Facilitating Mainstreaming through Cooperative Learning." *The High School Journal* 72 (1989): 83–88.

Orfield, G. "Hispanic Education: Challenges, Research, and Policies." *American Journal of Education* 95 (Nov. 1986): 1–26.

Pogrow, S. "Challenging At-Risk Students: Findings from the HOTS Program." *Phi Delta Kappan* (Jan. 1990): 389–399.

Pritchard, R. J. "Special Students in Regular Secondary Classes: Selected Annotated Bibliography." *Journal of Teacher Education* 35 (March/April 1984): 51–54.

Rendon, L., and S. Taylor. "Hispanic Students: Action for Access." *AACJC Journal* (Dec./Jan. 1989/90): 18–23.

Reynolds, M. "Students with Special Needs." *Knowledge Base for the Beginning Teacher.* Edited by M. Reynolds. New York: Pergamon Press, 1989.

Ruben, B. D. "Human Communication and Cross-Cultural Effectiveness." *Intercultural Communication: A Reader.* Edited by L. Samovar and R. Porter. Belmont, CA: Wadsworth, 1988. 331–338.

Schorr, E. *Within Our Reach: Breaking the Cycle of Disadvantage.* New York: Anchor Press/Doubleday, 1988.

Shepard, L., M. L. Smith, and C. Vojir. "Characteristics of Pupils Identified as Learning Disabled." *American Educational Research Journal* 20 (Fall 1983): 309–331.

Slavin, R. E. *Cooperative Learning.* New York: Longman, 1983.

Sleeter, C., and C. Grant. *Making Choices for Multicultural Education.* Columbus, OH: Merrill Publishing, 1988.

Soldier, L. "Cooperative Learning and the Native American Student." *Phi Delta Kappan* (1989), 71: 161–164.

"Special Report on the Education of Native Americans." *Education Week,* August 2, 1989.

# Course Management

## COURSE OUTLINES

Because speech programs vary greatly, it is difficult to construct a course outline that will apply to all speech programs. Your speech course will be determined by a number of factors.

1. Is the course a semester or a full year in length?

2. Is it a required course or an elective?

3. Is the course taught to a single grade level or a combination of grade levels?

4. Are the students in the class ability-grouped?

5. What is your own philosophy about the goals of a speech course?

The answers to these questions will determine the course you construct.

The suggested course outlines can be adapted to fit your particular situation. For example, a speech course that emphasizes interpersonal communication focuses on Chapters 1–8. Students will spend a great deal of time working in small groups and engaging in activities that will help them get to know themselves and others. A course that emphasizes public speaking and debate focuses on Chapters 9–15. A course that emphasizes performance skills might focus on Chapters 7–18. Students would perform several small-group discussions, public speeches, debates, and oral interpretations.

### COURSE OUTLINE FOR A ONE-SEMESTER SPEECH COURSE

*First Six Weeks*

| | |
|---|---|
| Communication Process (2½ weeks) | Chapters 1–4 |
| Communication and Self (1½ weeks) | Chapter 5 |
| Communication with Others (2 weeks) | Chapter 6 |

*Second Six Weeks*

| | |
|---|---|
| Group Communication (2 weeks) | Chapters 7 and 8 |
| Public Speaking (3 weeks) | Chapters 9–12 |
| Informative Speaking (1 week) | Chapter 13 |

*Third Six Weeks*

| | |
|---|---|
| Persuasive Speaking (2 weeks) | Chapter 14 |
| Debate (1 week) | Chapter 15 |
| Oral Interpretation (1½ weeks) | Chapters 16 and 17 |
| Group Interpretation (1½ weeks) | Chapter 18 |

## COURSE OUTLINE FOR A ONE-YEAR SPEECH COURSE

*First Six Weeks*
Communication Process (6 weeks)                Chapters 1–4

*Second Six Weeks*
Communication and Self (3 weeks)               Chapter 5
Communication with Others (3 weeks)            Chapter 6

*Third Six Weeks*
Group Communication
   Background (3 weeks)                        Chapter 7
   Forms (3 weeks)                             Chapter 8

*Fourth Six Weeks*
Public Speaking (4 weeks)                       Chapters 9–12
Informative Speaking (2 weeks)                  Chapter 13

*Fifth Six Weeks*
Persuasive Speaking (3 weeks)                   Chapter 14
Debate (3 weeks)                                Chapter 15

*Sixth Six Weeks*
Oral Interpretation
   Individual (2½ weeks)                       Chapters 16 and 17
   Group (3½ weeks)                            Chapter 18


## CLASSROOM CLIMATE

Much of the learning that occurs is a result of the communication climate teachers create in the classroom. Particularly in a communication classroom, where students will be asked to perform or demonstrate a behavior, a supportive classroom climate is essential. The climate must facilitate and encourage risk taking, exploring new strategies, and making mistakes. Students need to feel comfortable with each other and with you. This is particularly important as our classrooms become more culturally diverse.

The communication climate—either supportive or nonsupportive—begins the first day. For this reason, several initial icebreaking activities were included in this *Teacher's Manual*. Each is designed to help students get to know one another. It's important that students understand the purpose for the "getting acquainted" exercises. You might say something like, "During this course, you'll be discussing your ideas and feelings about many subjects with me and the other students in this class. In order for this to be comfortable, we need to know something about each other so we can build an atmosphere in which to share our thoughts. For the first several days of the course, we will begin each class period with an activity designed to help us get to know one another."

In addition to the icebreaking activities, you may also wish to establish some communication rules for the classroom that will help students feel supported. Some suggestions include:

1. Only one person may talk at a time.

2. Students may not ridicule another student's comments or writings.

3. Students are expected to listen to both teacher and student comments.

A final important aspect of a supportive communication climate is the model of a competent communicator that you as teacher provide. A teacher's verbal and nonverbal communication is noticed continually. Teachers can't expect students to listen to them if they don't listen to students; to discuss feelings if they do not share their own; to interact if they do not.

# Assessment

## MEASURING STUDENTS' PROGRESS

Students' communication can be assessed in several ways, from teacher observation to standardized tests. The assessment of oral communication is not an easy task, because it depends on the purposes and characteristics of the communicator, the topic being discussed, and the situation in which the communication occurs.

One thing is clear, however; assessment in a speech communication class must include much more than student performance on written exams. It is not enough for a student to list and define the duties of a small-group leader. The student must demonstrate her or his ability to perform those duties when called upon to lead a small group.

In addition, many communication skills are not easily measured on a teacher-made written exam or on a standardized test. Common objectives for a speech class are to build self-esteem, become more aware of and sensitive to the communication of others, and accept responsibility for individual communication. Affective objectives such as these cannot be assessed using traditional forms of testing.

The key to effective assessment in a speech class is to use a variety of assessment procedures and to match the procedures to the objectives. Certainly, a student's knowledge of content can be assessed using a paper-and-pencil test. That is why these kinds of tests are included in this *Resource Book* in Unit IV, Section C. However, assessing student performance also requires observation. A student's ability to apply the concepts learned to her or his everyday experience can be assessed by evaluating journal entries: sample assessment forms are included in Unit IV, Section A of the *Resource Book*.

Also included are assessment instruments for listening, interviewing, group discussion, oral interpretation, group interpretation, and public speaking skills. Some of these forms are for self-evaluation by the students; others are for peer evaluation. Still others are for teacher evaluation.

In addition to evaluating individual students' accomplishments on specific tasks, you should assess student progress. Measuring ability prior to, during, and following instruction can be particularly helpful in assessing those communication skills that are not easily measured objectively. For example, a common objective such as "build self-esteem" can be assessed by progress reports. You might assess this by having students complete a self-report measure (like that found in Chapter 5 of the text) periodically during the course. Scores can be compared from the beginning of the course to the end.

In addition to the specific assessment forms included in Unit IV, Section A of the *Resource Book,* you might want to use a more generalized checklist, which can provide greater flexibility. With such a form, you can record a student's completion of each objective in a chapter or unit simply by checking the appropriate box when the objective is evaluated. Since these competencies will be observed over the course of a unit of instruction, using a date in the box provides for more accurate records. During one two-week period, three or four specific skills might be evaluated. Later in the unit a different set of competencies are evaluated. For example, in the following table, the student named John Bond completed objective number 1 on April 5 and objective number 3 on April 15, and has not yet completed objectives 2 and 4.

| Objectives for Interpretive Reading | John Bond | Cathy Davis | George Ehrens | Mary Marquardt |
|---|---|---|---|---|
| 1. Choose appropriate material for oral presentation. | 4/5 | 4/5 | 5/3 | 5/6 |
| 2. Analyze literary selections. | | 4/8 | 5/6 | |
| 3. Perform selections as an individual or group. | 4/15 | | 3/10 | 5/6 |
| 4. Establish criteria for evaluation. | | | 5/15 | |

Another way to use the checklist is to record the extent of competency achieved. This can be done using a rating system such as:

0 = Not Observed
1 = Needs Work      *or*      − 1 = Below Average
2 = Average                    0 = Satisfactory
3 = Above Average              1 = Above Average

Regardless of which means of assessment is used, care must be taken in evaluating oral communication competencies. Perhaps only supportive comments should be given on a student's first try at a new competency. Negative criticism can come later—after a student has gained some confidence. The emphasis should always be on the performance of the student, not on her or his personality. Students need to understand that even though their performances may have been less than stunning, they are still good persons.

The Speech Communication Association has recently published *Guidelines for Developing Oral Communication Curricula in Kindergarten through Twelfth Grade* (available from SCA). This booklet outlines guidelines for each grade level and discusses some assessment criteria. The focus of the curricula is communication competencies for each grade level.

## CHAPTER REVIEW MATERIALS

### THINK ABOUT IT

The Think About It section at the end of each chapter requires students to review the text material. The questions are at a basic knowledge and understanding level. They do not require students to analyze or synthesize the text material. The Try It Out and Put It in Writing activities are designed for these purposes. Thus, answers to these questions are easily found in the text and have not been reproduced in this *Teacher's Manual.*

### TRY IT OUT

Many of the Try It Out activities involve role plays. Role plays enable students to experience the learning objectives rather than just reading and studying about them. In other words, role plays enable students to apply what they learn. Role plays are, perhaps, one of the best instructional tools for helping students become competent communicators.

When using role plays as an instructional tool, several ideas should be kept in mind.

1. Role plays are more than entertainment. Although students enjoy role plays, they should never lose sight of the major purpose of role plays—to act out real-life situations and analyze their own behavior and that of others.

2. Role plays are most effective when the classroom climate is supportive. To begin, you might have students role play in small groups rather than in front of the class. As students become more comfortable with this instructional technique, they can role play in front of the entire class.

3. Role plays have no scripts. In other words, the situation and characters are clearly defined for students, but students create the words and actions.

4. Role plays, to be effective, require observers. Assign some students as observers who will describe what they observed in relation to the objective of the role play. For example, what did they observe that contributed to the effectiveness of the communication in the role play?

5. Role plays should always be followed by an evaluation session. Both observers and role-play participants should take part in the evaluation session. Questions such as the following should be discussed.

- What happened during the role play?

- What helped make the communication effective or ineffective?

- How did the participants feel during the role play?

- What did we learn that we can apply to similar situations?

Many of the Try It Out activities require a significant amount of class time. You will need to be sure you have allowed ample time in your course planning. An activity that requires a performance by every student, such as small-group discussion, public speaking, or oral interpretation performances, will take considerable time. To help ensure every student is allowed time for performance, follow these guidelines.

1. Set a maximum time limit for student presentations and keep time during the performance. (You may wish to designate students to act as timekeepers.)

2. Allow time for oral critique or feedback. For each student speech of five to seven minutes, a good rule of thumb is three minutes per student. Fifteen minutes should be allowed for group discussion or group interpretation performances. In your critiques and evaluations, follow the guidelines for good critiques discussed in the text, and make sure students follow the guidelines when they critique fellow classmates.

3. Calculate the time necessary for the above activity and divide the remaining lost time by the maximum amount of time you have allowed for each presentation. Schedule the number of presentations or the length of a single group presentation. For example, if each student and critique time is one minute per student and you have twenty-five students in your class, you'll need twenty-five minutes for feedback. If the class period is fifty minutes long, and you allow five minutes for "housekeeping chores," you have twenty minutes for presentations. Dividing twenty minutes by three (the maximum length of time for each speech) tells you that you can listen to and critique six speeches each day. To complete all twenty-five student speeches, you'll need at least four days of class time.

   The same procedure should be used for each activity. Whether it is a formal speech activity, or a more informal report to the class, you'll need to describe how much time you will allow for each one.

When the Try It Out activities involve students working in small groups or dyads, remember to observe students closely to make sure they stay on track. As discussed previously, students often do not use group time efficiently or effectively without some prodding from the teacher.

Sometimes you will need to do some preparation before assigning the Try It Out activities. For example, Activity 2 in Chapter 6 asks students to discuss stereotyping and give a personal example. You might begin by giving a personal example yourself.

When students are asked to brainstorm topics or ideas, such as Activity 3 in Chapter 7, you will need to list a few ideas to get students started. The same is true when students are asked to select a topic for discussion or public speeches, such as Activity 4 in Chapter 8. Additionally, when students are asked to bring an item to class, such as an advertisement (Activity 4 in Chapter 13), demonstrating how to approach the activity by bringing in an item yourself can be beneficial. Finally, when students are asked to choose a proposition, or topic, such as Activity 3 in Chapter 15, you might bring a list of three or four sample propositions from which students can choose. Often material for such activities is listed for you in this *Resource Book*.

Some activities may be somewhat threatening to students; for example, making a collage of self and presenting it to the class (Activity 4, Chapter 12 or Activity 1, Chapter 5). To encourage students, you might do the activity, too, by preparing a collage about yourself and presenting it to the class before students are asked to present theirs.

## PUT IT IN WRITING

Remember that students are not accomplished writers and that they are often writing on topics they have never thought about previously. Make sure students understand the criteria for grading their written assignments. For example, students are often instructed to include the writing assignments in their journals. Share with them the journal evaluation form that you have chosen from this *Teacher's Manual*.

Offer constructive suggestions for improvement. Also, give students an opportunity to rework the assignments based on your suggestions. The goal is for students to build their skills. Reworking an assignment they have not done well can aid their skill building.

## SPEAK ABOUT IT

The goal of activities included in these sections is to help students gradually build public speaking confidence and skills. Thus, by the time they reach the public speaking unit, they will feel quite at ease.

In terms of evaluating these activities, choose one or two criteria and make sure students understand the criteria. For example, if a student is asked to give a one-minute speech defining an abstract word, evaluation might focus on whether or not the student used a clear example.

Focus your comments on ways students can improve their public speaking skills. Limit these suggestions to one or two for each assignment. Otherwise, students could become discouraged.

# Notes

1. Barbara Wood. *Development of Functional Communication Competencies: Grades 7–12.* Urbana, IL: ERIC and Speech Communication Association, 1977, p. 2.

2. James McCroskey. "The Problems of Communication Apprehension in the Classroom." *Communication Education* 26 (1977): 27–33. See also, James McCroskey, *Quiet Children in the Classroom.* Urbana, IL: ERIC and Speech Communication Association, 1991.

3. The material in this section is adapted from Pamela Cooper, *Speech Communication for the Classroom Teacher,* 4th ed. Scottsdale, AZ: Gorsuch Scarisbrick Publishers, 1991. 304–316.

4. J. Condon. "The Ethnocentric Classroom." In *Communicating in Classrooms,* J. M. Civikly, ed. San Francisco: Jossey-Bass, 1986. 11–20.

5. B. Bowman, "Educating Language-Minority Children: Challenges and Opportunities." *Phi Delta Kappan* (Oct. 1989): 118–120.

6. L. Barna. "Stumbling Blocks in Intercultural Communications: A Reader." In L. Samovar and R. Porter, eds. Belmont, CA: Wadsworth, 1988. 322–330.

7. B. Roe, E. Ross, and P. Bums. *Student Teaching and Field Experiences Handbook.* Columbus, OH: Charles E. Merrill, 1984. 187–188.

8. R. Slavin and W. Madden. "What Works for Students at Risk: A Research Synthesis." *Educational Leadership* (Feb. 1989): 4.

# TEACHING
# SUGGESTIONS

## Part One
## The Basics of Communication

The key to successfully teaching this course is building a supportive communication climate, one in which students will feel comfortable communicating. Building the climate begins on the day the class begins—with Part One.

Much time and effort will be needed during Part One to set the tone for all future units. Encourage students to talk. Share your ideas and feelings with them. For example, take part in any of the "getting acquainted" or "getting started" activities you assign. If you ask students to complete the checklist on page 8 of Chapter 1, complete it yourself and share your answers with the class. To create a supportive climate, follow these guidelines:

1. Avoid sarcasm and negative criticism.

2. Encourage all students, regardless of ability level.

3. Require students to listen to one another.

4. Model courtesy and respect.

5. Praise students.

6. Get to know your students' names quickly.

7. Interact with students as they work in pairs or small groups.

8. Solicit student comments and participation.

Since students often feel more comfortable talking to a single classmate than to the entire group, many of the Interact activities in this unit require students to pair off. Ask students what they liked, what they disliked, and what they learned from the activities.

When teaching Chapter 3 it is important to model good vocal production and good listening skills. If your speech is free from slurs, mumbling, and mispronunciation, and if your rate and volume are at a level at which all students in the classroom can hear and understand, students will more likely exhibit these vocal characteristics. If you listen attentively to student contributions, without interrupting, students will be more likely to exhibit good listening skills.

Because this part includes four chapters and provides the basis for the remaining parts, it will be extremely important to provide numerous examples for the various concepts taught. In addition, the relationships among the concepts need to be emphasized. References to or comparisons with prior or future learning will facilitate transfer. For example, a discussion of the importance of listening (Chapter 3) as it relates to the five communication acts (Chapter 4) would help students focus on the process idea of communication (Chapter 1). Showing students the relationships among these four chapters (or soliciting the relationships from students) will provide them with the necessary basics for successfully moving forward to the next parts.

# Chapter 1
# The Communication Process

Chapter 1 emphasizes the role of communication in a student's everyday life. *Communication* is defined as a process of sending and receiving messages in order to share meanings. Four types of communication—interpersonal, group, public, and interpretive are defined. In Chapter 1 students will learn to:

- Define *communication* as a process.
- Describe how communication skills influence family, school, work, and community life.
- Describe the four types of communication.

## WARM-UP

1. Have each student create a slogan by completing the statement "Communication is. . . ." Ask the class to vote for the best slogan as a class motto. As they learn more about communication, they may want to change the motto.

2. Have each student complete the Communications Checklist on page 8 of the text. Discuss with each student individually his or her responses.

3. Pair up students for "getting-to-know-you" interviews. Have each partner interview the other for five minutes (ten minutes for both interviews). Students may take notes. The following are suggested questions:

   - Where were you born?

   - Where have you lived?

   - Tell me about your family.

   - What are your hobbies?

   - Where have you vacationed?

   - What are your plans for this year?

   Have each student introduce his or her partner to the class, using the information from the interview.

# CRITICAL THINKING
# ACTIVITIES

## Communication Journal

### OBJECTIVE
To see how the four types of communication work in everyday life

### MATERIALS NEEDED
Communication Journal Suggestion Sheet ❏
Journal Evaluation forms ❏

### PROCEDURE
Ask students to keep communication journals during the course. As suggested in the text, encourage them to include a variety of items—news clippings, cartoons, poems, advertisements, photographs, slogans, drawings, and personal anecdotes. In order to get them started, distribute the Communication Journal Suggestion Sheet to each student. Ask them to use it as a guide. ❏

### FOLLOW-UP
Have students role-play the situations listed on pages 8–9 of the text. Ask them to discuss the role plays in their journals, focusing on how communication could have been improved in each of the role-played situations.

### ASSESSMENT
Journal Evaluation forms are included in Unit IV, Section A. Although it will not always be possible, an oral evaluation of the journals is appropriate. This might take the form of face-to-face conversations or tape recording your comments and giving the tape to the student.

Rather than collecting each journal assignment, collect the journals periodically. At times you may want to collect them without prior notice. Other times students could be given a due date on which a certain number of assignments are to be completed. ❏

### ENRICHMENT
Each chapter includes possible journal assignments in the Put It In Writing section at the end of the chapter. Many of these are appropriate for enrichment.

# Communicate This

### OBJECTIVE

To define *communication* as a process

### PROCEDURE

Instruct students to pair off. Ask one student to face the board and the other to face away from the board. Draw a figure on the board that is simple but not ordinary. For example:

Ask Student A, who is facing the board, to describe the figure to Student B. Student B must draw the figure on a piece of paper using Student A's *verbal* instructions only. Have students exchange roles, using a different figure.

### FOLLOW-UP

After all the students have had a chance to draw the figures, discuss with the class why communication is a complex process that requires eye contact, vocal cues, and gestures.

### ASSESSMENT

One of the Self-Evaluation forms in Unit IV, Section A may be used. ❑

### ENRICHMENT

Ask students the following question—How does communication today affect communication tomorrow? In the discussion that follows, emphasize the process idea of communication. Then ask students to write journal entries describing how their communication with a friend or parent is influenced by their past communication with that person.

# Communication Schedule

## OBJECTIVE

To describe how communication skills influence family, school, work, and community life

## PROCEDURE

Using the example below have students observe and record in their journals the number of hours per day they are involved in communication. Have them do this for one week.

| Time | Interpersonal | Group | Public | Interpretive |
|------|---------------|-------|--------|--------------|
| 7–8 A.M. | Mom wakes me. | | | |
| 8–8:30 A.M. | | Bus ride to school. | | |

## FOLLOW-UP

At the end of the week discuss in class the total number of hours each student spends. Write these on the board. Discuss the percentages of time spent communicating with family members, at school, at work, and in the community.

## ASSESSMENT

Check schedules for completeness.

## ENRICHMENT

Place the following chart on the board. Ask volunteers for answers.

| Place | People | Language | Dress | Topics Discussed |
|-------|--------|----------|-------|------------------|
| At home | | | | |
| At school | | | | |
| At a party | | | | |
| At a church service | | | | |
| At work | | | | |

Then ask students to consider some of the following questions. Do we communicate differently in different places with different people? How do past experiences with these people and places affect our communication and make it a process? What would happen if we tried to communicate the same way no matter where we were or who we were with?

# Ethical and Social Responsibility

## OBJECTIVE

To describe the ethical and social responsibilities of a communicator

## PROCEDURE

Have students role-play each of the following scenarios. Be sensitive to your students' situations in assigning the role plays.

### SCENARIOS

1. Your older sister yells at you after you have flunked a math test, "How could you be so stupid?" What is your response?

2. John is talking to Sally in a hall when his girlfriend, Sarah, walks up and glares at him. As soon as they're alone, Sarah screams at him, "How could you do that to me?" What is John's response?

3. Mario works at Burger King. Two hours before he is supposed to get off on Saturday night to go to a party, his boss asks him to work late. Mario sullenly says, "OK." What is the boss's response?

4. Two minutes after the bell rings, the English teacher says bluntly to Sue, "Your test is terrible. Evidently you didn't study." Sue glares at him and says, "Get off my back," under her breath. What is the teacher's response?

5. After sneaking her boyfriend into the house where she was babysitting Saturday night, Laura tells her best friend Patty on Monday morning and swears her to silence. By the next morning, six people have said to Laura, "I hear Bob was with you at the Bakers' on Saturday night." When Laura sees Patty at lunch, she says, "I thought I could trust you." What is Patty's response?

## FOLLOW-UP

After each role play, have students discuss the ethical and social responsibility of each person in the communication interaction.

## ASSESSMENT

Have students choose an Ann Landers or Dear Abby column from the daily newspaper. Then have them write short papers discussing the ethical and social responsibilities of the participants in each of the problems discussed in the column.

## ENRICHMENT

Students could write and read aloud poems or short stories about ethical and social responsibilities of communication.

# Chapter 2
# Elements of Communication

Chapter 2 defines and explains the elements of communication with an emphasis on nonverbal messages and perception. Verbal messages, noise in the channel, feedback, and context are also discussed. In Chapter 2 students will learn to:

- Define the elements of communication.

- Explain the categories of nonverbal communication.

- Describe the connection between verbal and nonverbal communication.

- Describe how noise in the channel affects communication.

- Describe how feedback works in the communication process.

- Watch a communication event and label the parts of the communication process.

## WARM-UP ACTIVITIES

1. Have students form a circle. Pass an object (for example, a chalk eraser) around the circle. Ask students to imagine the object is a puppy, a hot potato, a balloon, a small child, or a heavy box. Using only body language, the students should treat the object differently for each new name it is given.

2. To demonstrate how people are affected by personal space, change the seating arrangements in your classroom. Watch student reaction. Then lead a discussion on students' reactions and feelings in response to the changes.

3. Bring to class any of the following books: Mitsumasa Anno's *Topsie Turvies: Pictures to Stretch the Imagination* (Weatherhill, 1970) or *Upside-Downers: More Pictures to Stretch the Imagination* (Weatherhill, 1971); David McCauley's *Black and White* (Houghton Mifflin, 1990). Ask students what they see in the pictures. Discuss why every student didn't see exactly the same thing.

# CRITICAL THINKING
# ACTIVITIES

## Communication Is . . .

### OBJECTIVE

To define the elements of communication

### PROCEDURE

Divide the class into small groups. Ask each group to create a skit that demonstrates the elements of communication. For example, a group might create a skit in which the message one person sends is misunderstood by the second person.

### FOLLOW-UP

Have each group perform its skit for the class and explain how the skit illustrates the elements of communication.

### ASSESSMENT

Evaluate the skits using the following criterion: Did the skit clearly demonstrate the elements of communication? Write down the basic elements students saw demonstrated in the skits.

### ENRICHMENT

Videotape some of the skits and put together a program to show to other classes.

# Speaking Nonverbally

## OBJECTIVE
To explain the categories of nonverbal communication

## PROCEDURE
Give students the following directions for preparing a pantomime:

1. Select an event in your life that is simple to describe but involves several actions. For example: catching fish or frying eggs.

2. Before you perform your pantomime, ask yourself, "What must my audience clearly understand in order to fully appreciate what I am describing nonverbally?"

3. Practice each step of your activity before a mirror.

4. Time yourself. Do not take more than three minutes.

5. Perform your nonverbal description for the class, using as many categories of nonverbal communication as you can.

6. In your journal evaluate how well you performed each category of nonverbal communication for the class.

## FOLLOW-UP
Have volunteers describe what each pantomime was trying to communicate and what categories of nonverbal communication were used.

## ASSESSMENT
Evaluate students' performances on their attention to detail and utilization of nonverbal categories.

## ENRICHMENT
To help students understand that nonverbal messages can have several meanings, ask students to suggest what the following actions might mean.

- a person who keeps playing with a lock of hair
- a person who keeps his arms folded
- a person who drags her feet when she walks
- a person who has no expression
- a person who is stiff
- a person who slouches over
- a person who walks fast or swings arms
- a person who keeps biting his nails
- a person who keeps shaking her head no and looking down

# Seeing Is Not Believing

## OBJECTIVE
To describe the connection between verbal and nonverbal communication

## PROCEDURE
Show a videotape of a TV program, or a segment of a program, without the sound. Ask students to describe the plot of the show. Replay the tape with the sound.

## FOLLOW-UP
Focus classroom discussion on the connection between verbal and nonverbal communication. How did the verbal help understanding of the nonverbal and vice versa? Did misunderstanding occur when only the nonverbal was seen?

## ASSESSMENT
Ask students to write a short paper describing a communication event in which they participated and how verbal and nonverbal communication were connected.

## ENRICHMENT
Have a nonverbal day. Inform students ahead of time that no verbal communication will take place. The day before divide students into two groups. Have each group prepare clues for charades, using animals or names of famous people. On Nonverbal Day ask groups to switch clues and act them out. The audience cannot respond verbally but must write in large letters on pieces of paper what their guess is. Performers shake their heads yes or no. As a follow-up activity assign students a two-page report that answers the following questions:

1. How did Nonverbal Day make you feel? (frustrated, upset, happy)

2. What categories of nonverbal communication were used? Be specific.

3. How did you feel when you left class?

4. Give examples of how you communicated with other students.

# Nonverbal Emotions

### OBJECTIVE
To introduce how nonverbal communication is used to express emotions

### MATERIALS NEEDED
Slips of paper with an emotion listed on each

### PROCEDURE
Place slips of paper on which you have written emotions into a hat. Each slip of paper should contain one emotion—for example, happiness, doubt, disgust, interest, frustration, confusion, anger, love, sadness, joy, anxiety. Each student chooses a slip of paper and pantomimes the emotion. Classmates try to guess the emotion being portrayed.

### FOLLOW-UP
Ask students to explain what cues were most helpful to them in determining the emotions portrayed, and why.

### ASSESSMENT
Although pantomimes could be assessed for clarity, this activity is one that needs no formal assessment.

### ENRICHMENT
Students should watch a talk show host or news commentator for two weeks. During this time they should observe the nonverbal communication of this person—voice tone, rate, quality, volume, facial expressions, gestures, and manner of dress. Each student should write a description of his or her chosen person. If two or more students have chosen the same person, they could compare their findings. In their journals, students should write the description and what they believe are problems in the person's nonverbal communication.

# Nonverbal Cues

### OBJECTIVE
To use nonverbal cues to predict verbal messages

### MATERIALS NEEDED
Cartoons from newspapers and magazines with verbal messages and captions removed

### PROCEDURE
Give each student four or five cartoons. Have students write whatever dialogue or caption is suggested by the nonverbal message and share their captions/dialogue with other students.

### FOLLOW-UP
Discuss with students how the verbal messages they wrote support the nonverbal messages. Students can compare their captions and dialogues to those of the originals.

### ASSESSMENT
Ask students to write a short-answer essay explaining how nonverbal communication can support verbal communication.

### ENRICHMENT
Students should go to a busy mall or store and notice a difference in dress among the clerks and customers. Have students pick a few different styles and write a short paragraph describing them in their journal. Have students discuss what each of the different styles suggested to them about the particular person.

# It's So Distracting

## OBJECTIVE
To describe how noise in the channel affects communication

## PROCEDURE
Using the chart below, ask students to record and analyze the noise around them for the next twenty-four hours.

| Source of Noise | Could I Control Noise? | Effect on Communication |
|---|---|---|
| | | |

## FOLLOW-UP
Have students analyze the most common sources of noise in their communication and how it affects their communication by summarizing their findings in a one-page report.

## ASSESSMENT
Assess the noise analysis chart and the report using one of the Journal Evaluation forms in Unit IV, Section A. ❏

## ENRICHMENT
Have small groups of students compile lists of the most common sources of noise. Ask them to suggest ways of eliminating or controlling the noise.

# Oh, You Meant . . .

## OBJECTIVE
To describe how feedback works in the communication process[1]

## MATERIALS NEEDED
Dominoes—set of five for each student

## PROCEDURE
Divide the class into groups of five or fewer students, and let each group choose its own speaker. Arrange the dominoes for the speaker (refer to the diagram for a suggested pattern), and the game begins. Ask the speaker to study the domino arrangement. With his or her back to the group, the speaker is to instruct the members of the group on how to arrange their dominoes. Beginning with the top domino, the speaker should describe each in succession, taking particular note of the placement relationship of each to the preceding one. No questions are allowed. Different arrangements for each group will prevent eavesdropping. When a speaker finishes instructions to the group, compare the listeners' arrangements with one another and with the speaker's original pattern. Discuss similarities and differences.

Repeat the activity. This time listeners can ask questions and the speaker should face the listeners.

## FOLLOW-UP
After a class discussion about the importance of feedback (how speakers felt not being able to give it; how listeners felt), build a model of the communication process. Identify speaker, listener, message, feedback, sources of communication problems, and so on.

## ASSESSMENT
Evaluate the communication model. Does it contain all the elements of communication?

## ENRICHMENT
Share the communication model with other classes.

# I Know What I Saw

## OBJECTIVE

To watch a communication event and identify the parts of the communication process

## PROCEDURE

Stage a confrontation in your class with another teacher. For example, as you begin to use the overhead projector, have another teacher come in, demanding to use it immediately. Reasoning doesn't help and the teacher leaves—with or without the projector (you decide).

## FOLLOW-UP

Ask for written answers to the following questions.

1. How was the faculty member dressed? Does he or she wear glasses? What colors was he or she wearing?

2. Was he or she carrying anything?

3. What time did he or she come into the room? How long did he or she stay?

4. What started the disagreement?

5. Describe the actions and voices of the persons involved.

Have students read their answers aloud and identify the parts of the communication process. Have students listen for the points of difference and the areas of agreement. Discuss the reasons for the differences.

## ASSESSMENT

Have students tell how accurate they feel their own reports are. For instance, how would each person rate her or his answers on a scale of "absolutely sure" to "really couldn't say for certain"?

## ENRICHMENT

Ask each student to analyze a fairy tale from one of the following viewpoints—as a lawyer, doctor, teacher, sibling, parent, or friend. Have students read their analyses aloud. Discuss what about each person would affect perception.

## Notes

1. Adapted from Barbara S. Wood, ed. *Development of Functional Communication Competencies: Grades 7–12.* (Annandale, VA: Speech Communication Association, 1978), pp. 15–16.

# Chapter 3
# The Work of Speaking and Listening

Too often students confuse listening with hearing. Chapter 3 explains the differences. Listening is discussed as a four-step process. Chapter 3 identifies barriers to listening and explains guidelines for good listening. The chapter also discusses the vocal mechanism and the importance of the voice to effective communication. In Chapter 3 students will learn to:

- Describe the steps in vocal production.

- Define *listening*, and distinguish it from *hearing*.

- Describe the four steps in the listening process.

- Describe three barriers to good listening.

- List the guidelines for good listening.

## WARM-UP ACTIVITIES

1. Take the students for a walk around the school (stressing the importance of their remaining quiet). The students will record all the sounds they hear. When you return to the classroom, have students share their lists with each other. Discuss what noises were evident in each list, and which sounds were heard by only a few. For example: bell ringing, lockers slamming, a dog barking in the distance, leaves rustling, or a fly buzzing.

2. Invite a teacher of deaf students to visit the class. Ask the speaker to discuss how deaf people communicate and "listen."

3. Inform the class that there will be one piece of inaccurate information in the day's lecture. Students who have done assigned readings and who listen should be able to point out the error at the end of class.

4. Write the following on the board and instruct students to copy it on a sheet of paper.[1]

   a. 1

   b. P.B.    M.B.    S.B.

   c. Chicago    Houston

   d. vote

   e.

Read the following information *only once* and ask students to follow directions.

a. Put a dot on the *i*.

b. You are a baby calf and haven't had any loving in a long time. Who would you go to? Papa Bull? Mama Bull? Sister Bull? Circle the correct one.

c. A plane was flying from Chicago to Houston. It crashed ten miles north of Houston. Where would you bury the survivors?

d. Write *vote*.

e. You are the pilot of an airplane. There are fifty passengers aboard. The seats are dark blue and the carpet navy. There are five flight attendants aboard the plane. Two are five years older than the pilot; the other three are two years younger. How old is the pilot?

*Answers*

a. The dot should be put on the *i*, not above it.

b. Papa Bull (P.B.) should be circled since there is no such thing as a Mama Bull or Sister Bull.

c. Survivors are not buried.

d. The word *vote* should be written, not printed as shown.

e. The age of the pilot is the age of the person taking the quiz. The key is the first word of the statement.

# CRITICAL THINKING ACTIVITIES

## The Loaded Sentence

### OBJECTIVE
To describe the steps of vocal production[1]

### PROCEDURE
Ask students to pair off and practice the following tongue twisters together until they have control over the sounds. (Additional tongue twisters can be found in Unit IV, Section B.) ❑

*Consonant cluster:*
Amidst the mists and fiercest frosts
With barest wrists and stoutest boasts
He thrusts his fists against the posts
And still insists he sees the ghosts.

*th:*
Take this one and that one, another one, too.
Put them together for Agatha's stew.
Then gather some others from either design.
And then all the fathers and brothers can dine.

*y following h and l:*
A huge human being named Hugh
Thought Houston a beautiful hue.
Its millions of streets
Made a billion retreats
Like a huge human hewed it for Hugh.

*l:*
A self-help program means to help yourself get healthy, wealthy, and wise.
A little ladle was in the middle of the table.
"Tell Me a Riddle" is a beautiful story by Tillie Olsen.

*oi:*
They appointed a king by anointing his head with oil.

*a as in bake:*
I'm afraid I haven't made it plain.
Your plane is made of cellophane.

*er* **as in** *herd:*
I never heard a word from Merle
But Merle's a pearl, the only girl
To nurse a bird without a curse
Or a nervous word
When the bird turned worse.[2]

## FOLLOW-UP

Discuss the problems students had, how they overcame them, whether the speed at which they talked made a difference, and the steps of vocal production.

## ASSESSMENT

On an objective exam, ask students to describe the steps of vocal production.

## ENRICHMENT

Have students bring other tongue twisters or problem sentences to class to share with their classmates.

# Vocal Quality

## OBJECTIVE

To understand how voice qualities can affect communication

## PROCEDURE

Ask students to listen to and think about the vocal qualities of well-known radio or television newscasters in the community. Students should write down the strengths and weaknesses of the person's voice and share them with the class.

## FOLLOW-UP

Have a class discussion on how effectively each newscaster delivers vocal messages and what improvements he or she could make.

## ASSESSMENT

Ask students to

1. Choose a passage or a poem, or use a passage in this text.

2. Read it aloud and record it.

3. Listen to the recording several times.

4. Evaluate the quality of their own vocal messages.

## ENRICHMENT

Ask each student to identify someone—a radio or television personality, a movie actor, a sports figure, or a political leader—whom he or she believes possesses a pleasing voice. Have students discuss in their journals the qualities that make their chosen person's voice pleasing.

# Building Block Bonus

## OBJECTIVE

To define *listening* and distinguish it from *hearing*[3]

## MATERIALS NEEDED

A set of blocks that can be divided into two identical sets

## PROCEDURE

Put each set of blocks on a separate table and position the tables so that work at one cannot be seen at the other. If necessary use a divider to obstruct vision.

Ask a student to sit at each table. One student is the leader, the other is the follower. The leader creates a block construction while giving oral directions for its reproduction; the follower listens to these directions and attempts to build an identical construction. The objective is for the two students to build identical structures.

There are three versions of the game, and they are to be played in the following sequence. In the first version, the leader gives oral directions. The follower remains silent as he or she attempts to follow those directions; questions and comments are forbidden. In the second version, the leader again gives directions. This time the follower may ask yes-no questions of the leader. In the third and final version, the leader and follower may talk back and forth freely as the leader gives directions. You may want to switch students for each version. Obviously, the third version is most likely to produce identical constructions.

## FOLLOW-UP

Discuss problems in communication from a listener's point of view. Focus on why listening is an *active* rather than a *passive* process. How did asking questions help students distinguish listening from hearing? At what points did communication break down? Why?

## ASSESSMENT

Ask students to write one-page papers discussing the ways they intend to improve their listening skills in the next three days. Ask them to write a follow-up page on their success or lack of success.

## ENRICHMENT

Ask half the class to take turns giving directions for some simple tasks such as sewing on a button, polishing shoes, finding a word in a dictionary, addressing an envelope, or driving a car. Ask the other half of the class to evaluate the directions and discuss the problem of confusing listening with hearing.

# Round Robin Storytelling

## OBJECTIVE
To describe the four steps in the listening process

## MATERIALS NEEDED
Story Starters (see Tongue Twisters and Story Starters in Unit IV, Section B) ❏

## PROCEDURE
Copy the story starters on 3 × 5 index cards. Have students sit in a circle. One student draws a story starter and begins telling the story. At some point he or she stops, leaving the story unfinished. The next student adds on to the story. Each student in the circle adds something to the story. The student who started the story must end it. Have each student repeat the previous student's last sentence before adding his or her own sentences.

## FOLLOW-UP
Discuss the four steps of the listening process as they are demonstrated in this exercise. For example, ask students to examine what happened when they stopped *listening* and only *heard* the previous student's words.

## ASSESSMENT
Ask each student to complete the Listening Checklist and Self-Analysis form. Have them include it in their journals. ❏

## ENRICHMENT
Have students ask teachers the following questions.

- What are the effects of poor listening on students' achievement?
- Do most students need to improve their listening ability? On what grounds do you base your answer?
- What is the most common listening weakness?
- How can students learn to be better listeners?

Ask the class to make a list of the answers. Focus on the differences in terms of grade level or subject matter taught.

# Let's Compare Notes

### OBJECTIVE
To practice effective note-taking skills

### PROCEDURE
This activity gives students an opportunity to practice and evaluate their note-taking skills during an actual class lesson. You may adapt this activity to any lecture classes that you give.

Ask students to review the material on effective note taking on page 50 of the text. Indicate to students that during the lesson you will stop periodically and discuss or compare the notes they have taken.

### FOLLOW-UP
When you stop your lesson and have students compare notes, discuss with them why they decided to take the notes they did, how they organized the notes, and what comments they wrote on their notes.

### ASSESSMENT
Have students review their notes after class as discussed on page 50 of the text. During the next class period, have them return the notes to you. Assess the notes for accuracy and quality of revision.

### ENRICHMENT
Repeat this activity throughout the term. There are many possible variations on this activity. Play a recording of a speech and have students take notes. Or have them take notes on a lecture they attend, turning their notes in to you afterward. During the public speaking activities, have students take notes on the speeches.

# The Quiet

## OBJECTIVE

To understand that we often don't hear much of what goes on around us

## PROCEDURE

Have students go to the quietest place they know. They should listen to all the sounds and list in their journals ones that they never really noticed before.

## FOLLOW-UP

Ask students to share what they learned about listening.

## ASSESSMENT

Grade journal entries using one of the Journal Evaluation forms. ❑

## ENRICHMENT

Suggest to students that humans are able to think almost five times faster than they can talk. As a result, we can sometimes predict what another will say next. Ask students if this has ever happened to them. How did it affect their subsequent listening?

Play parts of recorded speeches for your class. Stop the recording at a certain point and ask students to write down what they think will be said next. After some students have read their predictions, play the next part. Were the predictions correct? What clues led to their answers?

# Barriers to Effective Listening

## OBJECTIVE
To identify the barriers to effective listening and ways to eliminate them[4]

## PROCEDURE
In their journals, ask students to record situations in which they stopped listening and the barriers that affected them. They should record situations every fifteen minutes for four to eight hours. Put the following form on the board as a guide.

| Situation | Listening barrier | My response |
| --- | --- | --- |
| My mother asked me to do three errands. | Internal distraction— I was thinking about my algebra test. | I asked her to repeat. |

## FOLLOW-UP
Have students work in small groups to list ways to eliminate the barriers they found. Each group should appoint a spokesperson to report the group's findings to the class. Summarize the findings and suggestions at the end of the class period.

## ASSESSMENT
Evaluate the journal assignment using one of the Journal Evaluation forms.
❑

## ENRICHMENT
Have students list ways they can eliminate barriers. Make sure they list specific behaviors such as "Don't study with the radio playing." Have students do periodic progress reports, updating their listening effectiveness. You could also do one for each student, based on your observations. Meet to compare progress reports.

# Description of a Parade

## OBJECTIVE

To list and use guidelines for effective listening while listening to descriptions[5]

## PROCEDURE

Send four students out of the room. Bring one back in front of the class and read him or her the following description of a parade. Then call in the next person and ask the first to repeat the description. Have the second tell the third, the third tell the fourth, and the fourth give a final version to the class. Have the class take notes during the process, and then try to trace the evolution of the description.

> Did you hear about the parade? It was at least an hour and a half long and had all kinds of things in it. There must have been thirty or forty clowns, and one of those little cars they drive had a dozen clowns inside it. They all got out right in front of me. The animals were amazing too: eight elephants all decked out in cloaks and jewels and all walking single file through downtown. The high school marching band played, and a couple of other bands from out of town. I think there was a drum and bugle corps, too. Oh, but besides the elephants there were monkeys in cute little shorts and a bunch of trained poodles.
>
> There were also incredible balloons. They were so big I could hardly get my arms around them. The food was pretty mediocre, though. I got a hot dog that tasted kind of strange, so I only ate a couple bites. But it was a pretty amazing thing, compared to most parades I've seen.

## FOLLOW-UP

Discuss the limits of listening, particularly in regard to perception and expression. Also discuss how students used the guidelines for good listening as they participated in this activity.

## ASSESSMENT

Ask students to write a short paper about how they use the guidelines for good listening to be included in their journals. The paper should focus on one communication event they have been involved in and how they used the guidelines during the event. Use one of the Journal Evaluation forms to evaluate the paper. ❏

# Listening Composition

## OBJECTIVE

To demonstrate competence in reflective and empathic listening in a variety of interpersonal situations[6]

## MATERIALS NEEDED

Active Listening Verification Sheet ❑

## PROCEDURE

Ask each student to listen empathically to a friend, parent, grandparent, or sibling outside of class. The person who participates in this empathic listening activity should complete the Active Listening Verification Sheet. Students should be told that they will not receive credit for this activity unless the Verification Sheet is completed and included in their journals.

Based on the empathic listening activity, students should write a one- to two-page paper describing what happened. Students should address the following questions in their papers:

1. Explain whom you worked with and what you talked about.

2. Relate in as much detail as possible how your conversation went. Include the following.

   • What was said

   • How you both reacted and felt (be very specific here)

   • How the conversation ended

3. Explain the results of the activity. Did you end up agreeing? Compromising? Did someone win or lose?

4. What effect did the process have on the discussion or argument? Did it slow it down or speed it up? Did it help you understand each other's point of view? Did it make the problem worse? Were you able to state and understand feelings better?

5. How do you feel about the process of empathic listening? Do you think you will use it again? Why? If so, when?

## FOLLOW-UP

Have students share their papers in small groups, discussing the problems they experienced and how these problems could be resolved.

## ASSESSMENT

Provide personal feedback to each student by writing comments about his or her paper.

## ENRICHMENT

Have students work in pairs to practice using the rules for reflective listening. Explain to students that:

1. Each person must restate whatever the other person says that either expresses strong feeling or communicates important information.

   "What I hear you saying is . . ."

   "Let me make sure I have this right. You feel . . ."

   "You mean to say that . . ."

   "Are you saying . . ."

2. If your partner paraphrases your statement correctly, reply, "Yes, that's what I meant," and move on to the next part of your discussion.

3. If your partner paraphrases your statement incorrectly, reply, "No, what I was trying to say was . . ." and repeat the whole sequence until your feelings have been correctly restated. Only then should you move on.

# Student Listening Tests

## OBJECTIVE

To demonstrate awareness of effective skills in listening and note taking for academic achievement[7]

## PROCEDURE

Indicate that all students will create short listening tests that they will read to the class. The assignment includes writing a short story and three test questions about the story or information given. If students have trouble being original, they may use a short article from a newspaper. Stress that the test should be interesting and appropriate. Read a sample story and test questions and have the class call out the answers.

## FOLLOW-UP

To prevent listening overload, only five or six student tests should be presented each day. Tell the students to come to the podium and read slowly, expressively, and clearly. Indicate that the listeners should avoid distractions and concentrate on the speaker. Have students take notes during some tests and not others. After each student reads his or her story, asks the questions, and gives time to respond, have the student give the answers. The students are to correct their own papers and keep their answer sheets to add to each day. Discuss with students the difference in the test taking when they took notes and when they did not.

## ASSESSMENT

In evaluating the assignment, assign points for the story, questions, and presentations. Take off points if the test is poorly presented or given late. Do not collect the answer sheets. The exercise should make listeners aware of how effectively they listened.

The following example was written by a student.

> Sid ate Cheerios while scratching his ear with a black, chipped fingernail. When he finished, he stood up and viciously kicked his fat cat through the kitchen window. The cat, traveling at a velocity of thirty miles per hour, landed in the back of a green Ford pick-up truck. The driver of the truck, who was suddenly disoriented due to the unexpected mishap, lost control of his vehicle, ran a red light, missed a right turn, and crashed through a guard rail.

1. What traffic law was broken? (running a red light)

2. What was the name of the person who ate Cheerios? (Sid)

3. At what velocity did the cat travel? (thirty miles per hour)

## ENRICHMENT

Have the students include a question that requires some processing of information, thus requiring the listener to go beyond literal processing to reflective processing.

# TV Ads: Truth or Falsehood?

## OBJECTIVE

To demonstrate skill in critical listening by analyzing, evaluating, and responding to videotaped television advertisements

## MATERIALS NEEDED

Videotaped television advertisements
Journal Evaluation form ❑

## PROCEDURE

Videotape several television advertisements and play them in class. Explain to students that advertisements often use Monroe's Motivated Sequence (see below) to persuade.

1. Attention: Get the attention of your receivers.
2. Need: Explain the need for your proposal and relate it directly to your receivers.
3. Satisfaction: Suggest what can be done to relieve the problem or need.
4. Visualization: Help receivers picture the benefits of relieving the problem or need.
   a. Receivers look to the future positively—see advantages to solving problem.
   b. Receivers look to the future negatively—see difficulties if problem is not solved.
5. Action: Indicate what steps or actions your receivers can take to relieve the need.

Play one advertisement, stop the tape, and explain to students how the sequence was used. Replay the advertisement, and answer any questions students might have.

## FOLLOW-UP

Play each advertisement. Have students discuss how each advertisement used Monroe's Motivated Sequence—either explicitly or implicitly. Ask students why they would or would not buy the product advertised.

## ASSESSMENT

Play one final advertisement and ask students to analyze it by writing about it in their journals. Evaluate each journal entry using one of the Journal Evaluation forms. ❑

## ENRICHMENT

Have students create and videotape their own advertisements. In small groups, have students analyze and evaluate each ad.

# I Like/I Dislike

## OBJECTIVE
To demonstrate skills in empathic and recreational listening and responding by describing personal response to a media performance[8]

## MATERIALS NEEDED
Journal Evaluation form ❑

## PROCEDURE
As a class, view a ten-minute taped or live television program segment. After viewing the segment, instruct students who liked the segment to sit on the left side of the room and those who disliked it to sit on the right side of the room. In an alternating fashion, have individual students state opinions by saying: "I liked (disliked) it because . . ." Time permitting, view a new segment and repeat the process.

## FOLLOW-UP
Students should give at least three reasons for their opinion. If after discussion students wish to change their opinion, they can move to the other side of the room. Take a final count of student opinions.

## ASSESSMENT
Have students write a paper listing three reasons why they liked or disliked this activity. Their reactions can also be included in their journals and evaluated using one of the Journal Evaluation forms. ❑

## ENRICHMENT
Students could use the same activity to discuss a movie they have all seen, or a school assembly program.

# Appreciative/Critical Listening

## OBJECTIVE
To demonstrate skills in appreciative and critical listening by reporting personal responses to public performance of literature[9]

## MATERIALS NEEDED
Poetry or Prose Reading Evaluation form ❑

## PROCEDURE
Review the concepts of critical and appreciative listening. Contact a middle school or high school forensic coach and request videotapes of at least three forensic performances in the same interpretive event. Ideally the performances should be of the coach's best students in those events. (Many coaches now use videotape to help students practice their performances. Another alternative is to invite forensic students to perform in class where they could be videotaped or to obtain a tape of professional storytellers from an educational video library.) Before viewing the tape, distribute and discuss the Poetry or Prose Reading Evaluation form. Ask students to take on the role of a judge at a forensic tournament. Be sure to review vocal and physical aspects of delivery and list them on the board.

## FOLLOW-UP
Students will listen to and view the oral performances and record their observations on the Poetry or Prose Reading Evaluation form. Discussion should focus on whether or not they enjoyed the performances, as well as how effective they thought the performances were.

## ASSESSMENT
Collect each student's evaluation sheet. Write comments on the sheets and return them to the students.

## ENRICHMENT
Students might try prose or poetry reading themselves.

# Notes

1. Adapted from Fran Tanner, *Creative Communication,* Topeka: Clark Publishing Co., 1979.

2. From "Resource Materials for Speaking and Listening in the Secondary Language Arts Program" (Corpus Christi, TX: Corpus Christi Independent School District, 1985).

3. From "Resource Materials for Speaking and Listening in the Secondary Language Arts Program."

4. From Kathleen Galvin. *Listening By Doing Teacher's Guide.* (Lincolnwood, IL: National Textbook Co., 1985).

5. From *Listening By Doing Teacher's Guide.*

6. Adapted from *Classroom Activities in Listening and Speaking* (Madison, WI: Wisconsin Dept. of Public Instruction, 1991), pp. 154, 167–169.

7. Adapted from *Speech Communication Teacher* (Winter 1991): p. 5.

8. Adapted from *Classroom Activities in Listening and Speaking,* p. 47.

9. Adapted from *Classroom Activities in Listening and Speaking,* pp. 78, 85.

# Chapter 4
## The Competent Communicator

The distinction between communicating and communicating well is discussed in Chapter 4. Communication acts—sharing information, discussing feelings, managing persuasion, following social rituals, and using imagination—are explained. The four steps used by a competent communicator—thinking of strategies, selecting a strategy, acting on a strategy, and evaluating the strategy's effect—are also explained. In Chapter 4 students will learn to:

- Define a competent communicator.

- Describe the five communication acts.

- Provide examples of speaking and listening for each of the five communication acts.

- Explain the four competency steps and how a competent communicator uses each of them.

## WARM-UP ACTIVITIES

1. Have students work in pairs. Each student should prepare a compliment to his or her partner. Have students exchange compliments. Discuss the correct way to give and receive compliments. Ask how it feels to give and receive compliments.

2. Ask each student to choose a feeling about which to create a music or art show. Classmates can guess the feeling after seeing the presentation.

3. Show the first fifteen minutes of the film *Veldt* (Phoenix, B.F.A., 1979, color, 23 minutes). In groups of three, have students create endings for the film. Have each group share its ending with the class. Show the rest of the film.

4. As a class, read the children's book *Noisy Nora* by Rosemary Wells. Discuss how a person feels when he or she is ignored. What does the person do? Your class might want to write a poem similar to Wells's using the ideas discussed. Share the poem the class creates with younger children.

# CRITICAL THINKING ACTIVITIES

## Scavenger Hunt

### OBJECTIVE
To describe the five communication acts

### MATERIALS NEEDED
Quest Reaction form ❑

### PROCEDURE
Send groups of five to seven students on a scavenger hunt. Prepare a list of questions to be answered by students, as well as a list of items to be obtained. When this activity was performed with a group of high school students from Chicago, the following are some questions the group had to answer and some objects they had to obtain:

1. What year was the original Water Tower built? (not the shopping mall)

2. What year was the Great Chicago Fire?

3. Where was John Dillinger killed?

4. How did the Loop get its name?

5. Why is Chicago called the "Windy City"?

6. Get a matchbook from the Drake Hotel.

7. Get a shopping bag from Marshall Field's without buying anything.

Because these questions are a bit unusual and historical, students were forced to ask others if they knew the answers. In some cases they asked complete strangers; in other cases they asked the Office of Tourism. Thus, they began to develop all five communication acts.

### FOLLOW-UP
Have students complete the Quest Reaction form. Ask them to share their answers. ❑

## ASSESSMENT

Evaluate the Quest Reaction form for accuracy and completeness.

## ENRICHMENT

Ask students to choose the communication act they feel they have the most difficulty performing. Ask them to keep a record for one week in which they describe (1) when they used the act (the situation), (2) with whom, and (3) how well they performed the act. Did they improve? Why or why not?

# It's As Simple As . . .

## OBJECTIVE
To provide examples of the informing act[1]

## MATERIALS NEEDED
Instruction Evaluation form ❏

## PROCEDURE
Have students work in pairs. You may either assign a task or allow students to choose their own. Examples of tasks include constructing a Tinkertoy structure, doing origami, drawing a picture, playing a simple musical instrument, or working with a puzzle. The person giving instructions is not to show how to complete any part of the task or to assist in any way. He or she may only describe how to complete the task. The person completing the task may not ask a question about an instruction until he or she has attempted to complete the step based on the initial information given, unless the sender asks if additional information is necessary. After the task is completed, have students switch roles.

## FOLLOW-UP
The following questions might be considered during the discussion.

1. How did the sender's word choices affect the receiver's ability to follow the instructions?

2. Did the person giving information always say what he or she meant? What happened when he or she didn't?

3. What happened when instructions were given in the wrong order?

4. What types of feedback from the receiver caused the sender to give additional or different instructions?

5. Which procedure works more effectively: (1) giving instructions one step at a time, or (2) giving brief explanations of the finished product or an overview of terms and materials before giving step-by-step instructions? Why?

## ASSESSMENT
Have each receiver of instructions complete the Instruction Evaluation form. ❏

## ENRICHMENT

Have the class generate rules for giving directions. Sample rules might include the following.

- Give the listener an idea of what you will be directing him or her to do.

- Do not assume that the listener will know what to do.

- Order the steps.

- Treat the listener like a human being.

# Feelings

## OBJECTIVE
To describe feelings

## MATERIALS NEEDED
3 × 5 index cards (two for each student)

## PROCEDURE
A few days before you plan to do this exercise, give each student two 3 × 5 cards, and ask them to write on each card a situation that generates an emotion. Some examples might include getting an F on a test, getting an A on a test, getting chewed out by the coach, being turned down for a date, getting a date with someone you really want to go out with, having a fight with your best friend, or winning a contest. Tell students to leave their names off the cards. After the cards are completed, put them all in a box. On the day you plan to do the exercise, get the box out and ask each student (or as many as time permits) to come up, select a card from the box at random, then briefly act out the situation described on the card. Ask the rest of the class to describe the feelings expressed.

## FOLLOW-UP
The following questions might be considered during the discussion:

1. In what other ways might the emotions be expressed?

2. What nonverbal cues (voice tone, gestures, facial expression) are used the most in interpreting how someone feels?

3. What verbal cues (tone of voice, speaking rate) are used the most in interpreting how someone feels?

4. How do words and actions work together to help express and interpret emotions and feelings?

Have students discuss how they would feel in a similar situation to that being portrayed.

## ASSESSMENT
Informal assessment can be conducted by keeping account of the accuracy of the guesses made.

## ENRICHMENT

Have students role-play various situations and describe their feelings. Examples include:[2]

1. You complain to a friend about a teacher who has assigned a great deal of homework for tomorrow.

2. A friend has just called to cancel a date to go to a movie tonight. You talk to your mom about how you feel.

3. You worked late last night on a social studies project that was due today. When you get to class, you learn the teacher has decided the project is not due because too many students in the class have not completed it. Share your feelings with an older brother or sister.

4. Your parents have grounded you for a week because you returned a library book late. You have paid the fine and cannot understand why you have been grounded. Talk to a relative.

5. After finishing a book report, you leave it on the kitchen table. A younger brother accidentally spills milk on it. Talk to your dad.

6. Your best friend ignores you in the hall. Talk to another friend about it.

Students can also role-play any other problems that are of concern to the group.

# Understanding Feelings

## OBJECTIVE

To provide an example of the feeling act[3]

## PROCEDURE

Ask each student to bring to class a poem, piece of prose, drama, newspaper column, or magazine article that expresses his or her feelings. Have each student read the selection aloud, attempting to make clear the feelings. Emphasize creating a supportive climate by having students sit in a circle.

## FOLLOW-UP

After each reading ask the group what feelings they heard. Ask the reader why he or she chose the selection and what feelings he or she wanted the class to hear.

## ASSESSMENT

No evaluation is necessary for this activity since students have put themselves on the line by choosing personalized material and performing it for their peers. You might end the activity by asking them how they felt about expressing feelings and why it is difficult to express feelings.

## ENRICHMENT

Explain how haiku poetry is constructed. Have students write haiku in their journals expressing their feelings about peers, family, religion, or themselves. Publish the haiku in the school literary magazine or in a class booklet.

# Parental Persuasion

### Objective
To provide an example of managing persuasion[4]

### Procedure
Divide the class into pairs. Ask each pair to create a persuasive message asking a parent for either an increase in allowance or money for a special activity. The students should collaborate in each stage of developing the persuasive message.

### Follow-Up
Have pairs role-play their messages in front of the class. Have one student portray the adolescent/persuader and the other the parent/audience.

### Assessment
Evaluate the persuasive messages by determining if they were well organized and clearly stated. Students can help assess the impact of each message by telling which person—parent or child—they sided with in the role play.

### Enrichment
Divide students into groups of five to seven. Provide each group with three television or radio commercials recorded on audiocassette or have them watch a current ad campaign. After each group has listened to the commercials, have students discuss whether they were persuaded and why. Then have each group select a product or service they would like to sell. Have them write a commercial. Ask each group to select one representative to present the commercial. Record the presentation and play it back to generate discussion.

# Feelings Evaluation

## OBJECTIVE

To demonstrate skills for public expression of feelings by giving a speech on a topic of personal interest or concern[5]

## MATERIALS NEEDED

Feelings Evaluation form ❑

## PROCEDURE

Each student should select an experience he or she had with a teacher that made the student feel particularly good or bad. This may be an interpersonal situation, a particular assignment, or other classroom experience. It need not be a recent experience. Encourage students to think back to elementary school. Also ask that they not slander people known to the class.

Students should prepare and present to the class a three- to five-minute talk that addresses the following points:

- a description of the experience
- feelings during the experience
- causes of those feelings
- effects of those feelings

## FOLLOW-UP

The following questions might be considered during the discussion:

1. Were you able to sense the speaker's feelings? What moments were particularly expressive? Why?

2. If the feelings were negative, how might the people involved in the situation have acted differently to avoid the bad feelings?

3. In a way, being a student is your job, your current occupation. Can you imagine an adult work experience that might involve similar feelings?

## ASSESSMENT

Use the Feelings Evaluation form. ❑

## ENRICHMENT

Students should write in their journals a description of how it felt to give this speech, focusing on the question of how difficult it is to discuss feelings in public.

# Everyday Persuasion

## OBJECTIVE
To demonstrate skills of persuading in a variety of interpersonal situations

## MATERIALS NEEDED
Everyday Persuasion worksheet ❑

## PROCEDURE
Have students keep a communication journal for two days describing (1) situations in which they had to defend their point of view with evidence, (2) what evidence they used, and (3) the effectiveness of their defense and use of evidence. They should use the Everyday Persuasion Worksheets to record the information.

## FOLLOW-UP
Have students work together in groups of three. Each student chooses one incident to share. The partners help the student to evaluate the evidence he or she used.

## ASSESSMENT
Peers can assess peers. Each group member can write a one-paragraph evaluation of how effective he or she believes the other group members' persuasion was. Collect the worksheets.

## ENRICHMENT
Have students observe others and analyze how persuasion is used in a variety of everyday contexts. They could suggest reasons to explain why the persuasion was or was not effective.

# Social Rituals

## OBJECTIVE
To provide an example of the social ritual communication act[6]

## PROCEDURE
Ask selected students to perform the following role-playing situations while other class members observe.

1. Two people who used to be neighbors and best friends in elementary school meet. One friend moved to another city and is in town visiting relatives. The two meet in any of the following places: a restaurant (one is just arriving and is waiting for a table, the other is leaving); a department store; or the concession stand at a movie theatre a few minutes before the movie is to begin.

2. A teacher, parents, and a student gather in the teacher's office for an annual parent-student-teacher conference. The teacher is responsible for leading the meeting.

3. A boy arrives at the home of a girl he is dating for the first time. The girl's father answers the door and lets the boy in. The boy must wait a few minutes until the girl arrives. The girl's older brother is also home.

## FOLLOW-UP
1. Ask students to discuss the approaches the students took in each situation. Were they appropriate?

2. If more than one group of students participated in each role-playing situation, ask students to analyze the different approaches each group took. Was one more appropriate or effective than the other? Have students discuss their reactions.

3. Ask students to discuss their own experiences in similar situations. How did they deal with each? What would they do differently if given another opportunity?

## ASSESSMENT
Ask students to observe family members, teachers, friends, and characters on television and in movies for approximately one week to determine if there are social rituals that are standard in our culture. Have them list those they found, and explain their importance to our culture. (This can be done orally or in writing.)

## ENRICHMENT

Ask students to role-play the following occupational situations:

1. Waiting on a customer at a fast-food restaurant. The customer is in a hurry and complains that you are too slow.

2. Answering a telephone and taking a message for the boss who is out of the office. The caller has called several times, and the boss has continually "just missed" the caller.

3. A receptionist introducing a client to the boss. The client is early for the appointment.

4. Waiting on a customer in a shoe store. The customer has had quite a bit of difficulty making a selection, and you have shown her or him nearly every pair you have in stock.

The following questions might be considered during the discussion:

1. What types of behavior do we expect from people who wait on us in restaurants or stores?

2. What roles do we play as customers?

3. What jobs have you held thus far (baby-sitting, lawn mowing, etc.)? What role did social rituals play in dealing with your employers?

# Is It Socially Acceptable?

### OBJECTIVE
To demonstrate awareness of the importance of social ritual to human interaction

### PROCEDURE
Prepare several scenarios such as the following:

1. You pass an acquaintance in the hall. You say, "Hi, how are you?" The acquaintance stops and says, "You know, I'm really not so good," and describes in detail what a horrible day it has been.

2. You go to class and a substitute teacher is in the room. The substitute sits, reading the newspaper. The bell rings and the substitute continues to read.

3. You want to save a place at the cafeteria table, so you leave your books on the table while you go get your food. When you return to the table, another student has put your books on the floor and is seated at your place.

After you have read each scenario, ask students to describe what social ritual has been violated. How would they respond? What happens to communication when social rituals are violated? How do people feel?

### FOLLOW-UP
Have students work in small groups to brainstorm ways of salvaging violated social situations.

### ASSESSMENT
Ask students to cite examples from movies, TV shows, or their own lives of how important social rituals are to effective communication.

### ENRICHMENT
In their journals, have students write about a time they or someone else violated a social ritual. The description of the event should include how the violation affected the interaction.

# Mellow Tone on the Telephone

## OBJECTIVE
To make and receive telephone calls effectively[7]

## MATERIALS NEEDED
Mellow Tone on the Telephone evaluation form ❑

## PROCEDURE
Brainstorm about what students believe is good telephone etiquette. Follow this with student thoughts on what constitutes rude telephone behavior.

List the qualities mentioned for good telephone etiquette and rude telephone behavior in separate columns on a board or easel visible to the class. Have students prioritize the good behaviors from one to eight (or more) in order of importance.

## FOLLOW-UP
Have students role-play in pairs various situations that call for telephone etiquette; for example, dialing a wrong number, leaving a message on an answering machine, changing an appointment, complaining about a product or service, or calling directory assistance. Have each pair choose one situation to perform for the class. Have three students evaluate each pair using the Mellow Tone on the Telephone evaluation form. These evaluations will supplement your own.

## ASSESSMENT
After each role play, have students evaluate the etiquette of the caller and the person being called using the Mellow Tone on the Telephone evaluation form. Both student and teacher evaluations should be shared. ❑

## ENRICHMENT
After practicing telephone etiquette on the first day, students could stage mock telephone interviews with literary or historic characters.

# Telephone Conversations

## OBJECTIVE
To communicate effectively on the telephone

## MATERIALS NEEDED
Role Play Evaluation form ❑

## PROCEDURE
Have students work in pairs and role-play the following using the information on good telephone behavior from the text.

- reaching a wrong number
- leaving a message for a friend who is not home
- asking to speak to a friend when a parent answers the phone
- asking for information about a product in a store
- making an appointment with an orthodontist

## FOLLOW-UP
Students should evaluate and discuss the role plays using the Role Play Evaluation form. ❑

## ASSESSMENT
Assess the role plays using the Role Play Evaluation form. ❑

## ENRICHMENT
Divide the class into small groups. Each group should prepare a skit depicting telephone situations such as calling to say you cannot baby-sit on Saturday night as you had agreed to do, calling someone you just met to invite him or her to a party, calling a friend to apologize for an argument, calling your parents to say you'll be late, or calling a dentist to make an appointment. Encourage students to be creative in coming up with their scenarios. After each group presents its skit, classmates should discuss the strengths and weaknesses of the participants' telephone communication.

# Introductions, Please!

## Objective
To make and acknowledge introductions[8]

## Procedure
Ask students to role-play introducing themselves or another person. Appropriate situations include the following:

1. You are a new student at school and know only a few people. You are looking for a place to sit in the cafeteria, and the only empty seats are by people you do not know. Sit down next to them, introduce yourself, and make small talk.

2. You are with your father in the grocery store and see your math teacher, who is the meanest teacher you have. She says hello to you first and stops in the aisle. Introduce her to your father.

3. Your school is involved in a money-making project, selling candy door-to-door. Your next-door neighbors are new to the neighborhood. Introduce yourself and explain your purpose.

   Select two or three sets of students for each role-playing situation. Have one set of students leave the room while the other performs.

## Follow-Up
The following questions might be asked during the discussion:

1. Were there any differences in the approaches taken by the two groups? Could one approach be considered better or more acceptable than the other?

2. What are the standard procedures for introducing oneself or another?

3. How should one refer to parents when introducing them (Mr., Mrs., complete names)?

4. What embarrassing situations have you experienced in being introduced or in introducing someone?

## Assessment
Assess this activity using the criteria for effective introductions on page 80 of the student text.

## ENRICHMENT

Give students one or two additional situations that involve introductions, and have them prepare explanations of acceptable procedures and sample dialogue for the situation.

# Getting to Know You

## OBJECTIVE
To learn the correct way to introduce people

## PROCEDURE
Brainstorm with students about what they believe is the proper way to introduce people. Follow this with students' thoughts on what they feel is improper. List the qualities mentioned for proper and improper introductions on the board or on an overhead projector for all the students to view. Discuss what makes some people receive more respect than others (for example, age, sex, position).

## FOLLOW-UP
Instruct the class to participate and observe as each student is called upon to introduce:

- a teacher to a member in the class.
- a female classmate to a male classmate.
- a doctor to a friend.
- a male classmate to a male classmate.
- a captain to a private.

## ASSESSMENT
After each role play, students will evaluate each other using the criteria generated for proper and improper introductions. Students and teacher should share the evaluations with the class.

## ENRICHMENT
Have students observe introductions made on television or in person. Have students share their observations with the class.

# Calling All Manners

## OBJECTIVE
To identify bad telephone habits and discuss rules of etiquette for telephone use

## MATERIALS NEEDED
One or two telephones
Mellow Tone on the Telephone evaluation form ❏

## PROCEDURE
Have students work in pairs to perform the following:

1. Discuss in class telephone habits that they find irritating.

2. Discuss ways to deal with a salesperson on the phone that they do not wish to speak to.

3. Demonstrate the proper ways to speak into the phone and ask to talk to someone.

4. Demonstrate how to ask for a certain person when someone else answers the phone.

5. Demonstrate making a business call to a department store to discuss returning a new radio that has quit working after a month.

6. Demonstrate how to handle a call that comes at an inconvenient time.

## ASSESSMENT
Have students evaluate the pairs using the Mellow Tone on the Telephone evaluation form. ❏

## ENRICHMENT
Have a telephone employee come and discuss with the class the business of telephone communication; or tour one of the local telephone companies.

# Once Upon a Time

## OBJECTIVE
To provide an example of the imagining communication act

## MATERIALS NEEDED
A fairy tale of your choice

## PROCEDURE
Read a fairy tale to the class. Ask students to imagine what happens after the fairy tale ends. For example, in "Cinderella" what happens after Cinderella marries the prince? What happens to her stepsisters and stepmother?

## FOLLOW-UP
After students have listed several options for what happened, divide them into small groups. Assign each group one of the endings. The group should create a skit based on the ending and act it out for the rest of the class.

## ASSESSMENT
Ask students to evaluate their experience by listing three things they learned from the activity about their own imagination skills.

## ENRICHMENT
Perform the skits for another class.

# School Situation Role Play

## OBJECTIVE

To explain the four competency steps and how a competent communicator uses them

## PROCEDURE

Ask students to role-play each of the following situations:

> Three students have just received grades for their Introduction to Communication course and have gone to complain to Ms. Lankin. David received a C+, James received an F, and Don received a D. All three students feel they deserved better grades. Ms. Lankin says that the grades the students received were fair.

> Joan, Jack, and Sarita spoke to Dr. Brown, their school principal. The students claim that Mr. McCoy's classes are boring, his tests are impossible to pass, and that students don't learn anything in his classes.

## FOLLOW-UP

During the class discussion list on the board as many ideas for each competency step for each situation as possible. Have students role-play the situations again, using ideas they had not thought of originally. Compare these role plays with the previous ones:

1. Did the communicators exhibit competent or incompetent communication behaviors?

2. What other strategies might the communicators have chosen? Would these have been more effective?

## ASSESSMENT

In their journals, have students analyze the following situation according to the four competency steps.

> Your friend has two tickets to a rock concert. The concert will not be over until midnight. Your curfew is 11:00 P.M. You decide to talk to your parents about extending your curfew until 1:00 A.M. so you can go to the concert with your friend. How will you approach them?

## ENRICHMENT

Ask students to create their own role plays.

# I'm an Effective Communicator When . . .

## OBJECTIVE

To demonstrate awareness of the importance of verbal, nonverbal, and listening skills for developing communication effectiveness[9]

## MATERIALS NEEDED

Role Play Evaluation form ❑

## PROCEDURE

Have students role-play the following situations:

1. You and your best friend are arguing over the fact that your friend decided not to go with you to the concert because she or he has just been asked to go with someone else.

2. You are furious with a friend when you learn he or she is going to a party where there are bound to be alcohol and drugs. You know he or she wishes to attend because a lot of popular kids from school will be there. You decide to tell your friend how you feel.

3. Your two closest friends are having another fight. You are tired of them always fighting and later that day you decide to tell them how you feel.

4. You want to go to a movie that lasts until 11:00 P.M., but your mom and dad say you must be home by 10:00 until your next birthday. Your parents have just gotten home from a hard day's work. The movie is rated PG-13, and your birthday is in one week. Persuade your parents to let you go.

5. You are one of two band students who are selling candles door-to-door to raise money to pay for a band trip to Florida in February. The candles are ten dollars each, and you need only two more sales to win the award for most sales. You are at the door of an old man who is very rich but is considered tight with his money. He is also known to dislike children. Persuade him to buy two candles.

6. You are one of two student council members who approach the principal to ask permission to hold a dance after school. A very popular band has agreed to play for free, but the band cannot play during school hours. The school policy is no night dances. Persuade the principal to make an exception to the policy.

7. You have been invited to a college football game. Your parents say you must wait until you're a year older to go unchaperoned. This is a very important football game. The winner goes to the Rose Bowl and will be ranked number one in the nation. Tickets are hard to come by, and your friend has only two. Persuade your parents to let you go.

8. A police officer has caught you riding your bike after dark without a light and wants to call your parents. Your parents said they would take away your bike if you rode it after dark. You went to buy a new light, but the light you wanted was sold out. Persuade the police officer to let you go on your way without calling your parents.

9. Your favorite band is playing in the area, and you and your friends have tickets. However, your father says he must accompany you to the concert. Everyone else's parents are dropping them off and picking them up after the concert. Your friends don't want to sit with your dad. Persuade your dad to stay home or just drop you off.

10. You are baby-sitting and have been told not to have any friends over. After the children go to bed, the boy or girl you are crazy about calls and wants to stop by. Persuade him or her not to stop by, without giving the impression that you are not interested.

11. You have a T-shirt for your mom's birthday with a picture of your mom's favorite musician on the front. Upon returning home you learn your brother bought the exact same shirt. You take the shirt back to the store for a refund to find you have lost the sales receipt. The clerk needs the receipt to give you a refund. Persuade the clerk to refund your money without the receipt.

12. You see your friend riding a brand-new mountain bike. Your friend won't let anyone ride it because it belongs to his or her father. Persuade your friend to let you ride it.

13. You need extra help with a very important assignment. The teacher told you that if you needed help, you could come in after school. You can't come in after school because you have practice. Persuade the teacher to help you during the lunch period.

### Follow-Up

Discussion should focus on how the verbal, nonverbal, and listening skills affected the effectiveness of the communication.

### Assessment

Informal assessment can be made by assessing each student's ideas in the discussion and by evaluating the role plays using the Role Play Evaluation form. ❏

### Enrichment

Ask students to create a two-page analysis of their own effectiveness in verbal, nonverbal, and listening skills. The analysis can be included in their journals.

# Competent Communicator

## OBJECTIVE

To analyze competencies of different personalities by reading or viewing the play *Twelve Angry Men* by Reginald Rose, and then identify the effectiveness of a competent communicator

## MATERIALS NEEDED

A copy of the play or video of *Twelve Angry Men*[10]

## PROCEDURE

After reading or viewing the video of *Twelve Angry Men*, students should discuss who was the best communicator of the group. Which jurors were the least effective communicators? Students should discuss the social rituals that were followed or not followed by the jurors. Students will discuss the problem of the incompetent communicators that were on the jury and how they affected the process of reaching a just and fair decision.

## FOLLOW-UP

After the above discussion, ask students to discuss the following statements and share their opinions of the law:

> A person is innocent until proven guilty.
> A person must be guilty beyond reasonable doubt.

## ASSESSMENT

Have students describe in writing each juror's effectiveness as a communicator.

## ENRICHMENT

Schedule a visit to a courtroom. Ask students to write a report or present an oral report of their experience.

# Notes

1. Adapted from Pamela Cooper, ed., *Activities for Teaching Speaking and Listening: Grades 7–12* (Urbana, IL: ERIC Clearinghouse on Reading and Communication Skills, 1990).

2. Adapted from *Classroom Activities in Listening and Speaking*, p. 54.

3. From *Activities for Teaching and Listening: Grades 7–12.*

4. From *Activities for Teaching and Listening: Grades 7–12.*

5. Adapted from *Activities for Teaching Speaking and Listening: Grades 7–12.*

6. Adapted from *Activities for Teaching Speaking and Listening: Grades 7–12.*

7. Adapted from *Classroom Activities in Listening and Speaking*, pp. 62, 67.

8. Adapted from *Activities for Teaching Speaking and Listening: Grades 7–12.*

9. Adapted from *Classroom Activities in Speaking and Listening*, pp. 59, 114–115.

10. Available from Key Video (A Division of CBS/Fox Video), Industrial Park Drive, Farmington Hills, MI.

# Part Two
# Communication with Self and Others

Students often have difficulty seeing their teachers as real people. They seem surprised to meet teachers outside the school environment—at the grocery store, at a movie, or in church. This makes it extremely important that teachers share personal examples to explain the concepts in Part Two. Students will be more willing to share their feelings if you do the same. Yet, you set the tone for appropriate class disclosure.

Just as you will not want to share everything about yourself, neither will students. If they find an activity too uncomfortable, an alternative activity should be allowed. Ideally, any information a student discloses in journal assignments should remain between you and the student.

Although positive reinforcement is always important, it is extremely important in this Part because students will, in some respects, be putting themselves on the line. Reinforcement may be in the form of positive comments, eye contact, standing near or moving toward students as they answer questions or make comments, smiling, or using a positive tone of voice. The effect of such positive reinforcement is an increased attempt on the part of students to participate actively.

Sometimes students will become overly talkative when interpersonal communication and friendship are discussed. Friends are extremely important to students, and some students may barrage you with personal examples. The problem in this case is to keep discussions on track. Students should certainly be encouraged to contribute their ideas about and experiences with friends, but they also should be required to relate their examples to the concepts being discussed.

# Chapter 5
# Communication and Your Self

Self-concept in communication is explored in Chapter 5. The term is defined, its four parts are discussed, and guidelines for improving self-concept are included. *Self-esteem* is defined. The relationship of self-concept and self-esteem to communication is discussed. In Chapter 5 students will learn to:

- Define *self-concept* and *self-esteem.*

- List the four parts of self-concept.

- Describe physical, social, and intellectual sides of themselves.

- Describe how self-concept, self-esteem, and communication skills are related.

- List four of their communication strengths.

- List three areas of communication they need to improve.

- Describe ways to improve their self-concept.

## WARM-UP ACTIVITIES

1. Have students design T-shirts that reflect their attributes. Ask each student to explain and display her or his T-shirt to the class.

2. As a roll-call activity for one week, ask each student to say something positive about herself or himself.

3. Have students create cardboard-backed buttons that reflect their personalities. On an assigned day, students should wear their buttons to class. Have students discuss their buttons with three or four of their classmates. Do classmates see students as "fitting" their button?

4. Have students write an "I Am" poem, using metaphors to describe themselves.

   *Example*

   I am a snowflake.
   There's no one else like me.

   I am a jewelry box.
   Open me and find a treasure.

5. Have students write their names vertically on a sheet of paper. For each letter of their names, have them write a positive word or phrase that describes them.

   *Example*

   *J* olly
   *A* lways Talking
   *M* ischievous
   *I* ntelligent
   *E* nergetic

6. Complete the self-assessment scale at the end of Chapter 5.

# CRITICAL THINKING ACTIVITIES

## A Personal Seal

### OBJECTIVE
To list the four parts of self-concept

### MATERIALS NEEDED
Clay and paint

### PROCEDURE[1]
Have students create their own seals, either by designing symbols for themselves or by using their initials. Keep the design simple. If a student uses his or her initials in the seal, he or she needs to draw them in reverse. For example, a *B* would be written ꓭ.

1. *Clay stamps.* Form clay into a two-inch-high cylinder with a diameter of about one inch. Using a pencil or paper clip, dig a design into one end of the cylinder. Then dip this end of the cylinder in paint and print patterns on paper.

2. *Clay printing blocks.* Form clay into a square or rectangle as large as desired but about one inch high. Using a pencil or paper clip, dig a design on one side of the square. With a brush, cover the design with paint. Then put a piece of paper over the design and, holding it in place, pat it gently. When the paper is lifted, the design will remain.

### FOLLOW-UP
Have students share their seals in pairs or small groups. They should discuss why they chose their particular design to symbolize their self-concept.

### ASSESSMENT
On an objective test, ask students to list the four parts of self-concept.

### ENRICHMENT
Display the seals in the classroom.

# This Is My Life

## OBJECTIVE
To describe physical, social, and intellectual areas of self

## PROCEDURE
Give the students the following directions: Create a "This Is My Life" scrapbook. Include pictures of yourself showing how you've changed physically from birth to now. Ask each member of your family to tell you something about yourself as you were growing up. Write these down and include them in the scrapbook. You might also include old report cards, old party invitations, or drawings you made when you were very young. On the last page of your scrapbook, explain what you learned about yourself physically, socially, and intellectually that you didn't know before.

## FOLLOW-UP
Have students share their scrapbooks with partners or in small groups.

## ASSESSMENT
Write evaluations using one of the Journal Evaluation forms focusing on the student's creativity and willingness to share information. Note interesting things you learned about the student. ❏

## ENRICHMENT
Have students write scripts for their own autobiographical slide show. Ask them to write three or four paragraphs about themselves. They should include biographical information as well as their hobbies, favorite pastimes, and most exciting memories. Suggest that they draw illustrations (one for each paragraph) to go with their scripts. Nonartists can copy or trace book illustrations. Put each illustration on a piece of black construction paper to create a "frame." Have a class artist illustrate an introductory and concluding frame. Then, using a camera with slide film, photograph each one.

When the slides are developed, decide what order to put them in and have students tape record their scripts in that order. Students might also record music that they feel is representative of them and play it as the slide show is being presented. (This activity can be adapted to create autobiographical videotapes.)

# To Know Me Is to Love Me

## OBJECTIVE
To describe how self-concept, self-esteem, and communication are related

## PROCEDURE
Have students sit in a circle. Ask them to write their names on the top of a sheet of paper and send the paper around the circle. Have each student write one or two positive descriptions on the paper about every person. When the paper returns, each student should have anywhere from twenty to fifty positive descriptions of himself or herself. (Make sure you stress to students to only write positive comments. You may wish to scan the papers to make sure no hurtful comments have been written.

## FOLLOW-UP
After students receive their papers back, discuss the following questions:

1. Are there any descriptions that don't fit the way you see yourself?

2. Are there any descriptions that you felt were correct?

3. How do others' views of you affect your self-concept? Your self-esteem? Your communication?

## ASSESSMENT
Students should include the list of descriptive words in their journals and circle those they feel describe them and underline those they feel do not. They should also write a one-page paper indicating (1) how they felt about the descriptive words and (2) what effect the words had on their self-concept.

## ENRICHMENT
Give students the following directions:[2]

1. Identify three questions you could ask yourself and other people that might help you collect information about yourself.

2. Answer your three questions by writing your perceptions of yourself.

3. Select five people to answer your questions. Choose a variety of people such as a person in your immediate family, a teacher, a friend, a neighbor, and a grandparent. Record their answers to your questions.

| Questions | My perception of me | Others' perceptions of me |
|---|---|---|
| 1. What am I like when I don't get my way? | 1. I'm very quiet and try to act like it's all right, but inside I'm unhappy because I like to do things my way. | 1. MOTHER: You pout.<br>2. TEACHER: You take yourself out of the group activities.<br>3. BEST FRIEND: You argue till you get your way. |

Have students answer the following questions in their journals.

1. What are the similarities and differences between the perceptions the five people have of you and your perception of yourself?

2. Do you feel that your view of yourself reflects what you really feel, think, say, and do?

# Self-Analysis

### OBJECTIVE
To list four communication strengths and three areas for improvement

### MATERIALS NEEDED
Listening Checklist and Self-Analysis form ❑

### PROCEDURE
Have each student complete the Listening Checklist and Self-Analysis form. Based on their answers ask students to list four of their communication strengths and three areas for improvement. ❑

### FOLLOW-UP
Ask students to include their lists in their journals. Ask them to describe how they feel their strengths help them to be better communicators, and to identify specific behaviors for improving those areas.

### ASSESSMENT
Evaluate the journal entry using one of the Journal Evaluation forms. ❑

### ENRICHMENT
Periodically ask students to review the areas they said they wanted to improve and write brief progress reports in their journals.

# I'm Getting Better

## OBJECTIVE
To describe ways to improve self-concept

## MATERIALS NEEDED
Personal Goals Analysis form ❑

## PROCEDURE
Ask students to list three behaviors they want to change in order to improve their self-concept. Then have them describe what they perceive their behavior to be at this time for each of the goals they want to achieve. For each of the three goals, have them describe what they could do that might help change the behavior to what they want it to be. Ask each student to complete the Personal Goals Analysis form. Have students include the sheets in their journals. ❑

## FOLLOW-UP
In small groups, have students share their goals.

## ASSESSMENT
Evaluate using one of the Journal Evaluation forms. ❑

## ENRICHMENT
Repeat this activity periodically during the term. Ask students to discuss with you or in their journals how well they have attained the goals or how the goals have changed.

# Johari Windows

### OBJECTIVE
To increase students' awareness of self

### PROCEDURE
Have students draw their own Johari Windows. They may choose whether or not they want to share all or parts of their windows.

### FOLLOW-UP
Explain to students that although they may not want to share all of the information, you would like them to discuss in general terms (1) what kinds of things they are willing to share and why; (2) whether they feel uncomfortable sharing information about themselves; (3) under what circumstances they feel most uncomfortable or most comfortable; (4) what kinds of things they like to know about other people; and (5) how self-disclosure can improve communication.

### ASSESSMENT
Have students write two or three paragraphs describing themselves and include the descriptions in their journals. Assess the journal assignment using any of the Journal Evaluation forms. ❏

### ENRICHMENT
Have students write poetry (haiku or cinquain) describing themselves, based on the information they gained through drawing the Johari Windows.

## Notes

1. Directions for activities were adapted from <u>Discover Art Series</u> by Laura H. Chapman (Davis Publications, 1985).
2. Adapted from Sharon Ratliffe and Deldee Herman. *Adventures in the Looking Glass*. Lincolnwood, IL: National Textbook Co., 1972, pp. 85–86.

# Chapter 6
# Communication with Others

In this chapter, *interpersonal communication* is defined as sharing meanings in order to build and maintain long-lasting, important relationships. Characteristics of friendship, stages of friendship building, and the building blocks of empathy, constructive criticism, supportive messages, listening, and sharing personal feelings are discussed. In Chapter 6 students will learn to:

• Define *interpersonal communication.*

• Describe the six characteristics of friendship.

• Describe the four stages of friendship and the communication patterns at each stage.

• Define the six communication building blocks of friendship.

## WARM-UP ACTIVITIES

1. Have students complete the checklist on page 125 in the text. Tell them to put it in their journals. Later in the course, ask them to complete the checklist again and write a short paper describing any changes and why they occurred.

2. Divide the class into small groups. Have the groups discuss the qualities important to friends listed on page 124 of the text. If they had been asked to rank these qualities, would they have ordered them in the same way as people in the survey did? Why or why not? Are there any qualities not included in the list that they would include? What are they?

3. Discuss some friendships in literature. Sample friendships include:

   Jess and Leslie in *Bridge to Terabithia,* by Katherine Paterson (New York: Avon, 1977)

   Meg and Calvin in *A Wrinkle in Time,* by Madeleine L'Engle (New York: Farrar, Straus & Giroux, 1962)

   Kit and Hannah in *The Witch of Blackbird Pond,* by Elizabeth George Speare (New York: Dell, 1958)

   Ned and Mr. Scully in *The One Eyed Cat,* by Paula Fox (New York: Dell, 1984)

   Dicey and Mina in *Dicey's Song,* by Cynthia Voigt (New York: Atheneum, 1986)

4. To begin a discussion of stereotyping, ask students to bring potatoes to class. Have students name their potatoes and divide the potatoes into peer groups. One group will be the "in crowd," another the "shy or introverted crowd," and so on. Discuss with the class why certain potatoes were placed in different groups. What classifies a "popular" potato or a "nerd" potato? Lead the students into discussing stereotyping. What does a popular person wear? What does a scholarly person wear? What does a nerd wear? What does an athlete, musician, chess player, cheerleader, or class officer wear? How does stereotyping affect friendships?

# CRITICAL THINKING ACTIVITIES

## What Is a Best Friend?

### OBJECTIVE
To describe the six characteristics of friendship

### PROCEDURE
After discussing important characteristics of friendship, ask each student to make a "What Is a Best Friend?" collage, and share it with the class. Students could then list ten to fifteen of the most common characteristics found in the collages, relating each characteristic to communication.

### FOLLOW-UP
Based on their collages, suggest that students write cinquains on friendship in their journals. Have students then write paragraphs analyzing how communication affects friendship and relating the ideas directly to their cinquains.

### ASSESSMENT
Evaluate journal assignments using one of the Journal Evaluation forms. ❏

### ENRICHMENT
Have students write articles about friendship for the school newspaper or poems about friendship for the school literary magazine.

# Stages of a Friendship

### OBJECTIVE
To describe the four stages of friendship and the communication patterns at each stage[1]

### MATERIALS NEEDED
Stages of a Friendship form ❏

### PROCEDURE
Select two characters from a novel, TV show, or film, and explain how their relationship progressed from the first-meeting stage to the best-friend stage. Have students describe the communication that characterized each stage using the Stages of a Friendship form. ❏

### FOLLOW-UP
Have students share the information on their forms either in pairs or in small groups. Have students include the Stages of a Friendship form in their journals. ❏

### ASSESSMENT
Evaluate using one of the Journal Evaluation form. ❏

### ENRICHMENT
Divide the class into small groups. Have each group write a skit demonstrating the development of a friendship and perform it for the class. Ask students to observe how accurately the skits reflect communication patterns at each stage of friendship.

# Journal of Friendship

## OBJECTIVE
To express feelings about friendships through journal writing

## PROCEDURE
Assign students to write in their journals for several days about their feelings on friendship. Journal topics could include the following:

1. List characteristics of friendships (look over Chapter 6's list of qualities). What do you feel are the most important characteristics of a friendship?

2. What is important to you about friendships?

3. Is it easy for you to make friends? How do you feel on first meeting someone?

4. What is stereotyping? How does it affect friendships?

5. What are the qualities of a best friend?

6. In today's society, many teenagers join gangs. What do you think kids are looking for in a gang? Do you feel that they find true friendships? Explain your answer.

## FOLLOW-UP
Ask students to discuss their journal topics in class. They may share journal entries or discuss a topic generally with classmates.

## ASSESSMENT
Evaluate the journal by checking to see if students are keeping up with the topics. Grades should be based on whether or not the students are keeping their journals updated.

## ENRICHMENT
Have different community people visit your class and discuss friendship—for example, a youth minister who has good rapport with students; a counselor who knows the importance of friendships; a local law officer or official who deals with gangs; or a counselor from a local hospital or clinic who has knowledge of teens and their fears and problems.

# Friendship Is Like . . .

## OBJECTIVE
To recognize the value of friendship through use of similes and metaphors

## MATERIALS NEEDED
Colored poster board and markers

## PROCEDURE
Discuss similes and metaphors. This can be an interdisciplinary project with English. Discuss the importance of friendship and have students write four or five poems using similes and metaphors. For example:

> Friends are like seeds. When nurtured they grow; when neglected they die.

> Friends are like rubber bands. If you stretch them too far, they'll snap back at you.

## FOLLOW-UP
After all poems are written, ask students to form small groups and write the poems on poster board. Display the poems in class.

## ASSESSMENT
Have students include their poems in their journals. Then have them select a poem by a classmate to keep in their journals. The journal entry containing the classmate's poem should contain a brief explanation of why the selection was made.

## ENRICHMENT
Have students select different poems, and take them to a printer or print shop. Have the poems bound into notepads with a poem on each page. (Usually the cost can be absorbed by selling the pads at twenty-five to fifty cents each.)

# Stereotyping

## OBJECTIVE

To recognize that stereotyping is harmful to communication and friendship

## PROCEDURE

Discuss in small groups some of the labels you have heard other people use for the people in each of the following categories. Give two examples of each.

> overweight people
>
> teenagers
>
> blondes
>
> teachers
>
> politicians
>
> slum kids
>
> dropouts
>
> smart kids
>
> rich kids
>
> good-looking kids

## FOLLOW-UP

Discuss with students how stereotypes can hinder effective communication.

## ASSESSMENT

Have students share their observations of the activity in a one-page report and include it in their journals.

## ENRICHMENT

Have students view a movie or videotape that deals with stereotyping, such as *School Ties* or *Pretty in Pink*. Discuss the movie's interpretation of stereotyping and how it affects people.

# I Feel . . .

### OBJECTIVE
To practice the building block of sharing feelings

### MATERIALS NEEDED
I Feel . . . form ❏

### PROCEDURE
Have students complete the I Feel . . . form. ❏

### FOLLOW-UP
Ask for volunteers to share some ideas from their forms. Discussion should focus on (1) how students might better communicate feelings both verbally and nonverbally and (2) why it is so difficult to share feelings.

### ASSESSMENT
Have students include the I Feel . . . form in their journals. Evaluate using one of the Journal Evaluation forms. ❏

### ENRICHMENT
The Interact on page 140 of the text about listening for feeling statements can be used as an enrichment follow-up to this activity. Students could complete the I Feel . . . form again later in the course and write a paper analyzing how they have learned to better express their feelings. ❏

# I Hate to Say This, But . . .

## OBJECTIVE
To practice the building block of criticizing constructively

## PROCEDURE
Divide the class into small groups. Give each group one of the following situations. Ask students to (1) discuss how they would tell their best friend the information and (2) role-play the situation for the class.

1. Your friend is overweight.

2. You dislike his or her girlfriend or boyfriend.

3. Your friend is caught cheating on a test.

4. Your friend promised to meet you at a party but never showed up.

5. Your friend told another person a secret she or he had promised not to tell.

## FOLLOW-UP
Discuss the role plays in terms of the guidelines for constructive criticism. Would anyone from the other groups have handled the situation differently? Why or why not?

## ASSESSMENT
Evaluate role plays in terms of students' ability to demonstrate the guidelines for constructive criticism as discussed in the text.

## ENRICHMENT
Ask students to write and role-play situations similar to the ones used in this activity (1) following the guidelines for constructive criticism and (2) not following the guidelines. Focus later discussion on how students in the role plays felt when guidelines were followed and when they were not.

# Expressing Empathy

## OBJECTIVE

To practice the building block of expressing empathy[2]

## PROCEDURE

Write the following on the board:

| Person | Situation |
|---|---|
| a close friend | dog just died |
| your grandmother | is hospitalized for an operation |
| your sister | won the state swimming meet |
| your mother | is celebrating a forty-fifth birthday |
| a favorite cousin | is getting married |
| your brother | was fired from a good job |
| an employer | is moving to another city |

Have students match four of the people with four situations and write messages that they would put inside blank greeting cards. They might also illustrate them. The messages should show students' empathy with the situation.

## FOLLOW-UP

Have students share their messages orally and explain how each message shows empathy. If they illustrated their cards, have them explain why they chose the particular illustrations.

## ASSESSMENT

Have students turn in the cards to you with an explanation of how each card demonstrates empathy.

## ENRICHMENT

Have students create cards for friends, parents, siblings, or grandparents that express empathy for a particular situation. They can mail their cards if they wish. In their journals, ask students to comment about their feelings as they made and sent the cards.

# The New Job

## OBJECTIVE

To demonstrate skills in explaining and predicting outcomes or solving problems in interpersonal situations[3]

## PROCEDURE

Read or hand out the following scenario:

> Jamie has been hired to clean the yard of Mr. Brown, who is moving into a house in the next block. Jamie has tended to his own yard and those of several other people, so he is sure he knows just what to do. He has contracted to "clean the yard" for one set price. Mr. Brown seems pleasantly surprised by the price Jamie quotes. He tells Jamie that there are tools in the garage, and he gives Jamie the key. Mr. Brown then leaves town to pick up his wife and family. When he returns, Jamie has finished the yard and goes over to return the key and get his money. To Jamie's surprise, Mr. Brown is angry and tells Jamie, "You only did part of the job. I will not pay you until you have finished." Jamie is puzzled and embarrassed. He feels that he has done what he was hired to do because he has done what he always does for his other customers. What went wrong?

Divide the class into two equal groups. Name one group Jamie and the other group Mr. Brown. Have each small group confer. Jamie groups should decide what he did when asked to clean the yard for the moderate sum he quoted. Mr. Brown groups should decide what Mr. Brown expected when he asked Jamie to clean the yard.

## FOLLOW-UP

The following questions might be used during the discussion:

1. Why do you suppose Jamie and Mr. Brown did not agree about what the job was to cover?

2. How could they have avoided this misunderstanding?

3. What could Mr. Brown have done differently?

4. What could Jamie have done differently?

5. What indication was there before Jamie cleaned the yard that there might be some misunderstanding?

6. What did Mr. Brown mean by the phrase "cleaning the yard"? What did Jamie mean by the phrase "cleaning the yard"?

7. What should Jamie and Mr. Brown do to solve this problem?

## ASSESSMENT

Through class discussion, informally assess students' knowledge of problem-solving techniques and their ability to predict possible solutions.

## ENRICHMENT

Show students a videotape of a half-hour TV program or give them a short story to read. Show only part of the videotape or have students read part of the story. Ask them to predict how the communicators will solve the conflict. Show the remainder of the videotape or have students finish reading the story. Have students discuss how the solution shown is better or worse than their suggested solutions.

# Who Said That?

## OBJECTIVE

To demonstrate awareness of the importance of exercising personal responsibility in communication choices[4]

## MATERIALS NEEDED

Copies of *USA Today* "Voices from Across the USA" features

## PROCEDURE

Each edition of *USA Today* contains a feature, "Voices from Across the USA" in the "Life" section. It consists of seven answers to questions such as "Should there be a law to declare English the official language of the United States?" or "Do you think college tuition costs are too high?" With each answer is a picture of the speaker and a listing of his or her occupation, city, and state.

Select several sets of these "Voices" that deal with questions of interest to students. Cut the answers apart from the pictures, keying them on the back for later use. Tape the row of pictures on a legal-size piece of paper. Beneath each picture place a quotation. Mix up the quotations so that they no longer appear under the correct pictures. Label the quotations *A* through *G* and the pictures *1* through *7*. Write an answer key.

Break the class into groups of four and give each group copies of different questions and responses. Instruct students to determine who said what, and to be prepared to share with the class the bases for their decisions.

## FOLLOW-UP

During the class discussion after this activity, stress the following.

> how stereotypes often lead to wrong conclusions
>
> how pervasive stereotypes are
>
> how listening to each of the people would have been affected by stereotypes
>
> how stereotypes might have interfered with analyzing an audience made up of people like the speaker

Students will help by saying things such as "A minister wouldn't use a word like . . ."; "I can't believe a man (or woman, old person, plumber, and so on) said that!" or "He'd be against student financial aid because he's a farmer." This activity will work to interest students in the topic of stereotyping, making them aware of their use of stereotypes and sensitizing them to the impact of that process on their thinking and communication.

## ASSESSMENT

Have students write in their journals on the topic of stereotyping as it relates to their own lives. Have them describe an incident in which stereotyping led to problems in communication. Have them discuss their personal responsibilities to avoid stereotypes.

## ENRICHMENT

Ask students to role-play communication with each of the responders. How do stereotypes affect our communication choices? Evaluate role plays using Role Play Evaluation form. ❏

# Notes

1. Adapted from Kathleen Galvin and Cassandra Book. Workbook to accompany *Person to Person* (Lincolnwood, IL: National Textbook Co., 1990), pp. 62–63.
2. Adapted from Workbook to accompany *Person to Person,* p. 69.
3. Adapted from *Activities for Teaching Speaking and Listening: Grades 7–12.*
4. Adapted from *Speech Communication Teacher* (Summer 1988), p. 6.

# Part Three
# Group Communication

Begin this unit by discussing with students how small-group communication relates to interpersonal communication. It is important that they understand how the interpersonal skills they learned in the previous unit affect small-group discussion. Constructive criticism, sharing feelings, and honesty are all important to use when disagreeing with a fellow group member. Similarly, being supportive to other group members will make the group decision-making process more productive and enjoyable.

You may find that when students work in small groups your most difficult task is to make sure students do indeed work. Too often students use the work time for socializing. Students need clear instructions about what they are to do and how they are to go about doing it. One way to avoid problems is to circulate among the groups as they work. As you circulate, watch how groups are doing in terms of following the directions for the assignment that you have given. Evaluate individual students' group discussion skills, and answer any questions the groups may have. However, do not do their work for them!

During the class periods in which students work in small groups, don't let the period end without summarizing for students what they should have accomplished.

Several forms for evaluating small-group discussions are included in this *Teacher's Manual.* Share the one you choose with students so they know what you expect them to do. Leave enough time to evaluate the small group performances orally. Students can learn much from the critiques you provide their classmates.

Whether you choose to give oral, written, or a combination of both types of feedback, it will be important to abide by the rules of effective feedback. Effective feedback is specific rather than general. Telling a student "Your organization was ineffective" does little to help the student. What specifically was ineffective and what can be done to eliminate the problem? Effective feedback also is well timed. In general, the more immediate the feedback the better. However, there are situations in which feedback should be delayed, for example, if a student is not ready to listen. Effective feedback focuses on the behavior, not the individual.

# Chapter 7
## Communication in Groups

Groups and group discussion are defined in Chapter 7, and the characteristics of groups are presented. Leadership style and the duties of leaders are described. Students are presented with a sequence to follow when solving problems. The responsibilities of speaker and listener in small groups are discussed, as well as the concept of leadership and how to evaluate group discussions. In Chapter 7 students will learn to:

- Define *group* and *group discussion*.
- List steps in problem solving.
- Describe the duties of leaders.
- Describe speaking and listening responsibilities of small groups.
- Evaluate a small-group discussion.
- Describe the characteristics of small groups.

### WARM-UP ACTIVITIES

1. With groups of ten to twelve seated around tables, place a box of pasta—lasagna, manicotti, bows, wide and narrow spaghetti, wheels, curls, shells, and other pasta shapes—on each table along with glue or rubber cement. Ask each group to work together to create a symbol of the class. Allow about forty minutes. When all groups have finished, ask each to give an interpretation of its class symbol. Ask them to discuss how they worked together on the task.

2. Instruct students to bring in a variety of magazine pictures. Tack a long piece of plain wrapping paper to the board as if you were setting up a mural. Assign small groups of students portions of the mural and several pictures. Instruct them to build stories out of the pictures by gluing them in sequences on the mural. Remind each group that its section of the mural must *tell a story*. Allow groups to work for twenty minutes. Then ask each group to explain its mural. Focus discussion on how each group interacted to get the job done.

3. Break the class into small groups of three or four persons each. Use the Brain Teasers form. Give the class five minutes for this assignment.[1] The answers follow. ❑

|   |   |   |   |
|---|---|---|---|
| 1. | sandbox | 11. | knee on lights (neon lights) |
| 2. | man overboard | 12. | circles under the eyes |
| 3. | I understand | 13. | high chair |
| 4. | reading between the lines | 14. | paradise |
| 5. | long underwear | 15. | touchdown |
| 6. | crossroads | 16. | 6 feet underground |
| 7. | downtown | 17. | mind over matter |
| 8. | tricycle | 18. | he's beside himself |
| 9. | bilevel | 19. | backward glance |
| 10. | 3 degrees below zero | 20. | life after death |

4. Draw the symbol *IX* on the chalkboard. Ask students to make a 6 (six) out of the symbol with the use of only one line. (The correct answer is *SIX*.) Ask students to discuss the following questions:

How many interpreted the *IX* to be the Roman numeral for *9*?

What lessons for problem-solving can we draw from this exercise?

# CRITICAL THINKING ACTIVITIES

## Orange Peel

### OBJECTIVE
To define a *small group* and list its characteristics

### MATERIALS NEEDED
One orange for each small group

### PROCEDURE
Ask the class to form small groups. Give each group an orange. Tell them their task is to peel the orange. Here's the challenge. They are to get the peel off in one piece, or as few pieces as possible. They must keep passing the orange from group member to group member. No group member may keep the orange more than ten seconds. The winning group is the one that removes the peel in one piece or in the fewest number of pieces.

### FOLLOW-UP
Ask students how they felt when they had the orange. Was there pressure from other group members? Ask students if they really performed as a group. When did they become a group? What characteristics of groups did they display?

### ASSESSMENT
Evaluate students' understanding during the class discussion of this exercise.

### ENRICHMENT
Ask students to analyze three groups to which they belong. What characteristics make the groups? When did each group become a group? Have students share their analyses orally or in their journals.[2]

# Creating a Story

## OBJECTIVE
To describe the norms and roles of a small group

## MATERIALS NEEDED
Instrumental music selections or paintings and pictures

## PROCEDURE
Divide students into groups of five to seven members. Have students listen to instrumental music selections and create stories based on the mood set by the music. Or have them choose a painting or picture and write a story about it.

## FOLLOW-UP
Focus class discussion by asking the following questions.

1. What did you learn about working in groups?

2. What were the norms of your group?

3. Were any of these norms harmful to the group's progress?

4. What roles were played by various group members?

5. Which roles were especially helpful or harmful?

## ASSESSMENT
As you circulate among the groups, evaluate each group member's participation. What role did you see each group member play? Did students adhere to the norms of their group?

## ENRICHMENT
Ask students to choose two groups to which they belong and analyze the roles played by the group members and the norms of the group. Ask them to write analyses and include them in their journals.

# Cooking Up Solutions

## OBJECTIVE

To list and use the problem-solving steps[3]

## PROCEDURE

Here's a simple way to get your students thinking about solutions to world problems. Have them write a feelings recipe. One student wrote this recipe for peace.

> 2 pinches of faith chips
> 5 liters of friendship juice
> 2 smigits of fun powder
> 3 bundles of cooperation
> ½ truckload of agreement
> a couple chunks of promises
> 1 handful of compromise
> 2 dashes of love sauce

> Blend the faith chips and fun powder in a large bowl. Add friendship juice while stirring. Melt chunks of promises and mix them with cooperation, agreement, and compromise. Stir in a few dashes of love sauce and let sit for 3 minutes. Bake at low heat and do not make much noise; peace is fragile. For best results, serve tenderly.—*From the gourmet kitchen of Joey Lee*

To assign a feelings recipe, select a current news topic the class is studying or allow students to select their own.

## ASSESSMENT

In addition to their recipes, ask students to include a one-page paper listing the problem-solving steps and describing how they used the steps to create their recipe.

## ENRICHMENT

Compile the recipes and publish them in the school newspaper or have students create their own class "cookbook."

# Inventions

## OBJECTIVE

To engage in a problem-solving activity

## PROCEDURE

In 1873, when Chester Greenwood was fifteen, he invented earmuffs. He made oval loops out of baling twine, had his grandmother sew pieces of beaver fur and velvet on them, and hooked the loops to his ears. Have your students create inventions to solve problems they have. Have groups share their inventions with the class.

This project can be as elaborate as you wish. Every year New Jersey's Department of Vocational Education holds an invention contest for grades K through 9. Students must think of a problem, come up with a way to solve it, make sure the way doesn't already exist, and then actually build it—keeping a detailed log as they proceed. To help students get started, obtain a copy of *Inventions Wanted!* by Harry Goff (Rutland, UT: Academy Books, 1980). It lists over four hundred of the best invention ideas from the magazine *Mechanics Illustrated,* which ran a column entitled "Inventions Wanted."

## ASSESSMENT

Circulate among the groups as they work, evaluating each group's use of the problem-solving sequence. Evaluate the inventions on originality and ability to solve the problem.

## ENRICHMENT

Have an Invention Night for parents. Have students work in small groups to plan various parts of the Invention Night—making and sending invitations, scheduling the exhibit space, preparing refreshments, and setting up the inventions.

# Solving the Crime

## OBJECTIVE
To discover the difficulty of reaching a goal in an unstructured group

## MATERIALS NEEDED
Clues from Solve the Crime Clue Sheet, cut into strips ❑
Solve the Crime worksheet ❑

## PROCEDURE
Cut the Solve the Crime Clue Sheet into twenty-six clues and give each student a clue from the list. If necessary, add clues or give some students more than one clue.

Instruct students that the only way to share the clue in class is to read it aloud. No one may pass the clues around to read.

Instruct the students that they have thirty minutes to solve the crime and answer the following questions:

1. Who was murdered?

2. Who was the murderer?

3. What time did the murder take place?

4. Where did the murder take place?

5. What was the motive?

6. What was the murder weapon?

Be ready for a noisy classroom. Many students will talk at once, and many classes never solve the crime. However, this is a great learning tool for showing students that the participation of each of them is needed and that organization and structure will help them reach their goals.

## FOLLOW-UP
Share the solution to the mystery with the class:

1. Who was murdered? *(Mr. Kelley)*

2. Who was the murderer? *(Mr. Scott)*

3. What time did the murder take place? *(12:30 A.M.)*

4. Where did the murder take place? *(Mr. Scott's apartment)*

5. What was the murderer's motive? *(Mrs. Kelley and Mr. Scott were in love and wanted to get rid of Mr. Kelley.)*

6. What was the murder weapon? *(a knife)*

Allow the class to have a group discussion about why finding the clues and solving the crime were difficult. Did the group get organized? How? Did subgroups form? Did any leaders emerge? Why did they become leaders? Are leaders important in a group? What happened to clues that belonged to shy people or to outspoken people? How did the thirty-minute time limit affect the group? If the crime was not solved, what was the major factor preventing the group from solving it?

## ASSESSMENT
Ask students to write in their journals what they learned about working in groups. Evaluate the journal entries using one of the Journal Evaluation forms. ❑

## ENRICHMENT
Show students the beginning of a television murder mystery such as "Murder She Wrote" or "Columbo." Let them try to solve the crime by discussing the different clues provided in the program. See if the class can solve the mystery.

As an alternative, have students read a detective story (such as the stories of Arthur Conan Doyle), closing the book before they reach the end and trying to solve the crime before the story's detective does.

# The Martian Problem

### OBJECTIVE
To demonstrate group problem-solving techniques

### MATERIALS NEEDED
Martian Solution sheet for each student ❏
Martian Problem worksheet for each student ❏

### PROCEDURE
Provide students with copies of the Martian Problem worksheet. Give them five minutes to solve the problem. At the end of five minutes, divide the class into groups, and again give them five minutes to solve the problem. At the end of five minutes, call on one member from each group to present the group's solution. ❏

### FOLLOW-UP
Discuss the differences between individual and group problem solving. Then give students the Martian Solution sheet. ❏

### ASSESSMENT
Ask students to write in their journals about the differences between individual and group problem solving. Assess their answers using one of the Journal Evaluation forms. ❏

### ENRICHMENT
Ask students to solve more problems. One example: Connect all nine dots with only four straight and connected lines.

The solution to this problem is based upon the creative insight of going outside the obvious boundaries of the dots.

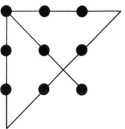

117

# Respect

## OBJECTIVE
To describe the duties of a leader

## MATERIALS NEEDED
Respect Discussion Sheet ❏

## PROCEDURE
Divide students into groups of five to eight and assign each group a leader. Have them discuss respect, using the Respect Discussion Sheet. Have each group present their conclusions to the class. ❏

## FOLLOW-UP
Write the duties of a leader on the board. Discuss whether these duties were performed in each of the groups. What happened to the groups if the duties were not performed?

## ASSESSMENT
Evaluate the discussion members and leader using one of the evaluation forms. ❏ Ask leaders to evaluate themselves using the checklist on page 176 of the text.

## ENRICHMENT
Similar lessons may be developed with topics such as self-discipline, fair play, ambition, and authority.

# The Squares Game

### OBJECTIVE

To describe the speaking and listening responsibilities of small groups[4]

### MATERIALS NEEDED

Squares and instructions for students
Small-Group Self-Evaluation form ❏

### PROCEDURE

Before class, prepare a set of squares and an instruction sheet for every five students. Divide the class into groups of five and seat each group at a table supplied with a set of envelopes and an instruction sheet. Ask that the envelopes be opened only on signal. Describe the experiment as a puzzle that can be solved only by cooperation.

Give the following instructions to students. Each person should have an envelope containing pieces for forming squares. At the signal, the task of the group is to form five squares of equal size. The task is not complete until everyone has a perfect square and all the squares are of the same size. The rules are the following:

1. No member may speak.

2. No member may signal in any way that he or she wants a card.

3. Members may give cards to others.

Give the signal to open the envelopes. When all or most of the groups have finished, call time and discuss the experience.

### PREPARATION OF PUZZLE

A puzzle set consists of five envelopes containing pieces of stiff paper cut into patterns that will form 6-inch squares, as shown in the diagram. Cut the squares into parts and lightly pencil the letters *a* through *j* as shown below. Then mark the envelopes *A* through *E* and distribute the pieces as follows:

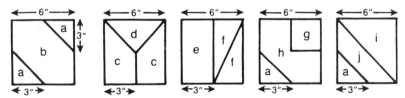

Envelope       A — j, h, e
B — a, a, a, c
C — a, i
D — d, f
E — g, b, f, c

Erase the small letters from the pieces and instead write the envelope letters *A* through *E* on the pieces so that they can easily be returned for reuse.

Several combinations of the pieces will form one or two squares, but only one combination will form five squares.

## Follow-Up

Focus discussion on the way in which students fulfilled their responsibilities as both speakers and listeners.

## Assessment

Evaluate the speaking and listening skills of each group member.

## Enrichment

Have students analyze their own communication using the Small-Group Self-Evaluation form. ❑

# Professional Insight

### OBJECTIVE

To demonstrate competence in verbal, nonverbal, and listening skills by participating in small-group discussions for the purpose of imparting information to an audience[5]

### MATERIALS NEEDED

Job Explanation Speech Evaluation form ❑

### PROCEDURE

Explain your job as a teacher, using two or three kinds of expository materials. Discuss the many jobs that are available in our society. Introduce the assignment, which is to present a two- to three-minute speech explaining the job of an adult known by the students.

Students are to interview the adult and record information for use during the next class period.

Have students work in groups to share information and decide which information to use in final speeches. Have students prepare note cards and practice in their small groups.

### FOLLOW-UP

Assign two listening checkers for each speech. Listening checkers will ask the audience questions about the speech to determine how well the audience listened.

Have students deliver speeches. Following each speech, invite questions from the audience.

### ASSESSMENT

Evaluate the student speeches, using the Job Explanation Speech Evaluation form. Have students write short papers analyzing how their verbal, nonverbal, and listening skills were enhanced through this activity. ❑

### ENRICHMENT

Use this activity as a springboard to a discussion of careers.

# Evaluating a Small-Group Discussion

## OBJECTIVE
To evaluate a small-group discussion

## MATERIALS NEEDED
Small-Group Discussion Evaluation forms ❑

## PROCEDURE
Choose six class members to discuss one of the following questions for ten minutes: What does *responsibility* mean? What makes a person educated? What are the characteristics of an effective school principal (or teacher)? Other members of the class should complete one of the Small-Group Discussion Evaluation forms. ❑

## FOLLOW-UP
Have students compare their evaluations.

## ASSESSMENT
Have students include their forms in their journals. Identify individual and group weaknesses.

## ENRICHMENT
As you assess your students' small-group discussion skills, consider long-term growth. For example, compare individual ratings from the beginning of the unit to the end to see if personal growth has taken place.

# Notes

1. From John Newstrom and Edward Scannel. *Games Trainers Play.* (New York: McGraw-Hill, 1980), pp. 76–77.

2. Patricia Baudendistel, Teacher's Edition of Kathleen Galvin and Cassandra Book, *Person to Person* (Lincolnwood, IL: National Textbook Co., 1985).

3. Adapted from Franny McAleer, "Let the Inventive Spirit Soar!" In *Gifted Children Monthly* (January 1985). Gifted and Talented Publications, Inc.

4. Adapted from *Classroom Activities in Listening and Speaking*, pp. 93–94, 99–100.

# Chapter 8
# Forms of Group Discussion

This chapter examines various forms of small-group discussion. Students are given information on committees, panel discussions, and symposiums. Parliamentary procedure is also discussed. In Chapter 8 students will learn to:

- Define *committee, panel discussion, buzz group, forum,* and *symposium.*

- Describe the roles of leader and participants in committee, panel discussion, and symposium.

- Define *parliamentary procedure* and its four principles.

- Describe the duties of parliamentary officers.

## WARM-UP ACTIVITIES

1. Check your TV program guide or radio listings for programs that use a panel discussion format. Educational television and local cable stations often give public service air time for local groups to discuss such things as bond issues. Videotape one of these programs for your class to view. Instruct students to analyze the discussion and the size of the group, seating, structure, and eye contact. How did each individual member's knowledge of the topic influence the discussion? How does leadership affect what the group is able to do?

2. Invite a parliamentarian from one of the service clubs in your area or from a local union to visit your class. Ask the guest to discuss the uses and problems of group decision making.

# CRITICAL THINKING
# ACTIVITIES

## Committee Recommendations

### OBJECTIVE
To participate in a committee

### MATERIALS NEEDED
Committee Evaluation form ❏

### PROCEDURE
Divide the class into five or six committees. Each committee should work on a common issue or problem of interest, probably school-related. You might use the topic in the text on new courses (see page 186). Each committee should meet to discuss its topic and try to determine the real problems, key issues, and possible solutions.

### FOLLOW-UP
Ask committees to report their findings and decisions to the class. Focus discussion on evaluating the findings of each committee and students' feelings about working on committees. Ask them what was most difficult and what was least difficult.

### ASSESSMENT
Have students engage in self-evaluation. They should focus on their communication strengths and weaknesses as a committee member. These evaluations should be included in the students' journals. Use the Committee Evaluation form. ❏

### ENRICHMENT
Have student committees report their findings to the school principal.

# The Members of the Panel

## OBJECTIVE

To prepare and present a panel discussion[1]

## MATERIALS NEEDED

Panel Discussion Evaluation form ❑

## PROCEDURE

Ask groups to prepare and present panel discussions. Make sure each group has a leader who will divert questions to the group members. Encourage the groups to prepare outlines of their discussion. Require that they present a brief practice discussion a few days before giving their final presentations.

## FOLLOW-UP

Discuss the panel discussions, focusing on the effectiveness of the leader and participants.

## ASSESSMENT

Use the Panel Discussion Evaluation form. ❑

## ENRICHMENT

You may want to have the class select the most successful panel discussion and arrange for this discussion to be presented in the community. Public libraries are often glad to receive such student presentations.

Have students present panel discussions for another class. Before they select their topics, have students interview members of the audience to determine their likes, interests, and concerns. Finally, have them plan and present the discussions. Invite students to share their reactions to interviewing the audience before preparing the discussions.

# Buzz Groups

## OBJECTIVE
To participate in a buzz group

## PROCEDURE
Ask for volunteers to role-play forum speakers. Then select one of the following subjects and assign roles to students. Give the forum members ten minutes to prepare. After they hold their forum, break into buzz groups for ten minutes.

### Subjects

- promoting school involvement in celebration of city's 75th birthday
- increasing school spirit at football games
- getting student volunteers for community organizations

### Roles

- history teacher
- student council president
- PTA president
- parent
- head cheerleader
- principal
- mayor
- city social worker
- football coach

## FOLLOW-UP
Focus discussion on the facts learned from the panel and forum, and the effectiveness of the buzz groups.

## ASSESSMENT
As buzz groups work, circulate among them. Note each member's willingness to contribute.

## ENRICHMENT
Ask students to evaluate the effectiveness of the buzz groups in short written papers to be included in their journals.

# Lecture Forum

## OBJECTIVE

To participate in a forum

## MATERIALS NEEDED

Forum Tabulation form ❏

## PROCEDURE

Invite a guest speaker to your class to present a fifteen-minute talk.

## FOLLOW-UP

When the speaker has finished, give the class twenty minutes to discuss the subject in open forum. General comments may be made, and questions may be asked of the speaker or of other members of the class who have spoken. One member of the class will serve as forum leader, one will be the group recorder, and three will serve as evaluators.

## ASSESSMENT

Use the Forum Tabulation form. ❏

## ENRICHMENT

In their journals, students should write their reactions to the lecture forum. Topics to be covered might include the communication effectiveness of the participants and an outline of the information students learned.

# Symposium Participation

## OBJECTIVE
To participate in a symposium[2]

## MATERIALS NEEDED
Symposium Evaluation form ❏

## PROCEDURE
Divide the class into symposium groups of five to seven students. Select one member of each group to serve as the leader. Give each group a choice of three topics. Once the group has chosen its topic, the group will divide the subject into important subtopics. The leader of the group will be responsible for seeing that each member of the symposium has a specific subtopic to present.

Give students two days to do library research and one day to organize their research. On the fourth day, the symposiums will begin. Each leader will present a two- to three-minute introduction of the subject, followed by an introduction of each symposium speaker, and that speaker's subtopic. As each speaker is introduced, that person will present a three-minute subtopic statement. When all the speakers have shared their information, the leader will give a two-minute summary of the symposium's findings.

## FOLLOW-UP
Following the symposium, focus class discussion on how effectively each symposium leader and members communicated and the advantages and value of this discussion format.

## ASSESSMENT
Use the Symposium Evaluation form. ❏

## ENRICHMENT
Assign four or five students as evaluators. They should each complete the Symposium Evaluation form. Have them lead a discussion on the effectiveness of the symposium and follow-up session. ❏

# Parliamentary Procedure

## OBJECTIVE
To utilize parliamentary procedure

## MATERIALS NEEDED
Parliamentary Procedure Participation Evaluation form ❑

## PROCEDURE
Have students conduct a class meeting according to parliamentary procedure. One person should act as temporary chairperson until the group elects a president. Then have students elect a vice president, a secretary, and a treasurer. Have students propose, discuss, and vote on motions about meeting days, class projects, field trips, or other activities that the class is involved in.

## FOLLOW-UP
Discuss the activity with the class. Focus on the importance of parliamentary procedure for orderly discussion. Have students relate their experience in this activity to the four principles of parliamentary procedure discussed in the text on page 193.

## ASSESSMENT
Use the Parliamentary Procedure Participation Evaluation form to rate students' participation. ❑

## ENRICHMENT
Play a tape of the movie *Mr. Smith Goes to Washington.* Focus class discussion on the roles and procedures of the Senate. What happened once someone had the floor? In these discussions did the rules help the meeting move toward a fair ending? What would happen if there were no order in the Senate and House of Representatives?

# Student Congress

## OBJECTIVE

To learn parliamentary procedure through a mock student congress

## MATERIALS NEEDED

Parliamentary Procedure Participation Evaluation form ❑

## PROCEDURE

Introduce students to the basics of student congress.[3]

Explain to students that they will need to present bills to class the next day. The bills should be brief, one-issue proposals about changes in school policy. For example:

> Students should be allowed a longer passing period between classes.
>
> Students should be allowed to leave campus during lunch.
>
> The varsity football team should be co-ed.

Bills should be written in the following form:

---

S.C. Bill— _____ student's last name _____ — #1

proposal _____

_____ student's signature _____

---

A sample completed bill will look like this:

---

S.C. Bill— _____ Johnson _____ — #1

That all students should be allowed to chew gum in school.

_Siri Johnson_

---

"S.C. Bill" means "Student Congress Bill." The number after the student's name indicates that this is the student's first bill. Students should sign their bills. Collect the bills and make copies for all students in the class.

Assign a student to serve as chairperson, or play the role yourself. The chairperson should call on students to present their bills. Bills must be moved and seconded, referring to the bill number (for example, S.C. Johnson #1 Bill). Once bills have been seconded, they are open for discussion and a vote.

There are several rules for student congress discussion:

1. Students should call each other "Senator" and use their last names.

2. Students must not speak until recognized by the chair. When speaking, students should stand.

3. Students should follow parliamentary procedure at all times, making motions and seconding them. (You should encourage students to keep their textbooks open to the chart on pages 202–203.)

The following is an example of parliamentary procedure at work:

CHAIR: I have several bills before me. Do I hear a motion to hear a bill? Senator Johnson?

SENATOR JOHNSON: I move to hear the S.C. Johnson #1 bill.

SENATOR SOUTH: I second the motion.

CHAIR: It has been moved and seconded to hear the S.C. Johnson #1 bill. Any discussion? All in favor say yes. All opposed say no. *(Pause.)* Senator Johnson has the floor.

SENATOR JOHNSON: I move that all students be allowed to chew gum.

SENATOR SOUTH: I second the motion.

CHAIR: Any discussion? Senator Johnson.

SENATOR JOHNSON: It is a known fact that we are old enough to chew gum. It is ridiculous that we are not given this privilege.

CHAIR: The chair recognizes Senator Garza.

SENATOR GARZA: It may be true what the senator says, but when she says "all students," then we can assume she means students in elementary school, too. I don't think first-graders should be allowed to chew gum in school. The teachers will have problems with the little kids getting it everywhere.

## Follow-Up

Discuss the activity with the class, focusing on the difficulties as well as the importance of following parliamentary procedure.

## Assessment

Use the Parliamentary Procedure Participation Evaluation form. ❑

## Enrichment

Have students attend a town meeting or a student congress or model United Nations session and observe parliamentary procedure in action.

# Notes

1. Adapted from Teacher's Edition for *Person to Person*.
2. "Resource Materials for Speaking and Listening in the Secondary Language Arts Program." Corpus Christi Independent School District, Corpus Christi, TX, 1985.
3. For more information about this forensics activity, you might consult David Mezzera and John Giertz, *Student Congress & Lincoln-Douglas Debate*, 2nd ed. (Lincolnwood, IL: National Textbook Co., 1989), or Linda Oddo and Thomas McClain, *Student Congress* (Lincolnwood, IL: National Textbook Co., 1994).

# Part Four
# Public Communication

Often students are apprehensive about giving public speeches. As we suggested earlier in this *Resource Book,* there are several things a teacher can do to lessen this apprehension. Before beginning Part Four, review the material on communication apprehension in the text.

Students need so much information before they can give a good public speech that it may seem difficult to know where to begin. This unit begins with simple speech situations and progresses to more difficult ones. When students follow the sequential steps we have set forth in the text, most will succeed very well. It is easier to apply the public-speaking skills to speeches of social ritual and informative speaking than to persuasion or debate. Thus, the chapters progress from least to most difficult speaking situations.

Critiquing speeches is not an easy task. Several evaluation forms are included in Unit IV, Section A of the *Resource Book.* Choose the one appropriate for your goals and your students. You may want to listen to the first few speaking assignments without critiquing each student individually. Instead, it may be better to give general critiques that apply to many students. You can then use these first few performances to diagnose each student's strengths and weaknesses and individualize the instruction accordingly.

When critiquing speeches, point out strengths and weaknesses, suggest how to eliminate weaknesses, and end with a positive comment on improvements you've noticed since the last speech performance. Critiques may be written or given orally. Whenever possible we suggest a combination of the two. Oral comments can help students learn from one another's mistakes as well as strengths.

Students should also critique one another's speeches. Remind students of the qualities of a good critique as discussed in the text (pages 326–327). Peer evaluation can be done in several ways. Students can volunteer to be a critic, or you can assign a group of students as critics for the day. You might assign one critic for each speaker. It is probably wise to vary these from day to day.

Students should also engage in self-evaluation. Following their speaking assignments, they should complete one of the Self-Evaluation Forms included in Unit IV, Section A of the *Resource Book.* Such self-evaluation can help them develop their self-concepts as well as develop public speech skills.

# Chapter 9
## Introduction to Public Speaking

Chapter 9 provides an introduction to public speaking and defines this important concept. Basic principles such as audience analysis, topic selection, purposes of public speaking, and audience goals are presented. In Chapter 9 students will learn to:

- Define *public speaking*.
- Give examples of situations in which people give public speeches.
- Describe the three main purposes of public speaking.
- Describe the guidelines for selecting a topic.
- Explain the importance of audience analysis.
- List four types of information needed for audience analysis.
- Define and create sample audience goals.

### WARM-UP ACTIVITIES

1. Assign students the presentation of impromptu speeches. These speeches should be one to two minutes in length. Have students draw topics out of a hat. Possible impromptu topics include:

   What is your pet peeve?
   What is a good teacher?
   What is a friend?
   What is honesty?
   What is homework?
   How would you spend $10,000?
   What advice would you give a student entering junior high?
   What is your ideal vacation?

2. Have students design individual coats of arms. (See form in Unit IV, Section A of the *Resource Book.*) The coat of arms should have at least three symbols, one each from the student's past, present, and future. More symbols may be used. Ask students to explain their coats of arms. ❏

3. Ask students to write cinquains and share them with the class. Discuss with the class how writing a cinquain compares to preparing a speech: choosing an interesting topic, organizing in three parts (introduction, body, conclusion), using supporting materials, relating the topic to themselves, and making the most of word choice.

# CRITICAL THINKING ACTIVITIES

## Everyday Public Speaking

### OBJECTIVE
To give examples of situations in which people give public speeches

### PROCEDURE
Have students interview a person who does a great deal of public speaking to determine how the speaker (1) uses public speaking in her or his career and (2) prepares to speak in public. Other teachers, administrators, school board members, attorneys, civic leaders, and politicians may be interviewed.

### FOLLOW-UP
Have students share the results of their interviews in brief oral reports. Following the oral reports, make a chart of all the interview results and place it on the classroom bulletin board.

### ASSESSMENT
Evaluate student oral reports based on organization and completeness of information.

### ENRICHMENT
Ask community persons who often speak in public to share their experiences with your class.

# Public Speaking Journal

## OBJECTIVE
To describe the three main purposes of public speaking

## PROCEDURE
Have students keep a record in their journals of the public speakers they see or hear. Students should record:

- Speaker
- Receiver(s)
- Purpose of the public communication
- Audience goal(s)
- Students' reactions to the public speaking event

You may choose to have students keep their journals for a limited period of time (for example, for one or two weeks) or for a more extended period of time.

After students have kept their public speaking records for the specified amount of time, have them compile their information into reports about the kinds and quality of public speaking events they have witnessed.

## FOLLOW-UP
Discuss the reports in class to demonstrate the importance of public communication in everyday life and the variety of purposes for public speaking.

## ASSESSMENT
Evaluate student reports for variety and understanding.

## ENRICHMENT
Have students keep a scrapbook of public communication activities, such as newspaper articles, magazine clippings, or pictures that illustrate principles discussed in class or presented in the text. Ask them to write a short paragraph for each example, identifying the source and indicating the purpose of the public speaking event illustrated. Students can also include in the scrapbook their feelings about public communication— its role in everyday life, their fears about it, and their reactions to text readings or class discussions.

# Choose a Letter

### OBJECTIVE
To describe guidelines for selecting a topic

### PROCEDURE
Have students choose a letter of the alphabet and flip through the dictionary under their chosen letter for potential speech topics.

### FOLLOW-UP
Ask each student to write out a list of topics. Collect and copy the lists to hand out to students. In small groups, have students choose two or three letters and decide on the best ten topics using the guidelines discussed in the text. Ask students to decide on a speech purpose and an audience goal for each topic.

### ASSESSMENT
Evaluate the appropriateness of the topics for classroom use and the appropriateness of the audience goal to the speech topic.

### ENRICHMENT
Ask each student to select a different letter and complete the exercise again, choosing at least four words. For each word the student should write in his or her journal an audience goal and a short paragraph describing why it would make a good speech topic.

# Audience Observation

## Objective

To explain the importance of audience analysis

## Materials Needed

Access to speech or speech videotapes

## Procedure

Have students observe a public speech. Instead of focusing on the speaker, ask them to focus on the audience. Was the audience interested? Bored? What behaviors indicated the audience's reaction? Did the speaker adapt to the audience? How? Why was the adaptation important?

## Follow-Up

Have students report their observations to the class. Each student could present a brief one- to two-minute speech telling (1) who the speaker was, (2) the audience's reaction, and (3) the speaker's adaptation to the audience's reaction.

## Assessment

Assess each student's speech, focusing on the student's organization.

## Enrichment

Ask students to observe several public speeches during this unit and write a short paper on each. The papers should include steps 1–3 under Follow-Up.

# It's the Audience That Counts

## OBJECTIVE
To list four types of information needed for audience analysis

## PROCEDURE
Have students begin working on speech topics of their choice. They should imagine they will give the speech to a group of third-graders, a group of high school juniors, the local PTA, or a group of senior citizens. Students should consider the characteristics of each group (age, gender, occupation, education), the purpose for each group, the beliefs and values of each audience, the group's knowledge of their topics, and how the students might create different audience goals.

## FOLLOW-UP
Have students prepare and present speeches on one of the topics for one of the audiences. Ask class members to role-play a designated audience.

## ASSESSMENT
Assess the speech using one of the public speaking evaluation forms in Unit IV, Section A. ❑

## ENRICHMENT
Have students present their speeches to the PTA, senior citizens groups, or other groups.

# Audience Goals

### OBJECTIVE
To define and create sample audience goals

### PROCEDURE
Ask students to imagine they will present the following topics to each of the listeners indicated. Students should formulate an audience goal, consider the information they would use, the order in which they would present the information, and the language and information they would use.

1. Explain the fun of roller skating to a four-year-old who has never skated, a teacher who thinks it's dangerous, or a friend who loves skiing.

2. Explain your new high-tech stereo system to your science teacher, your friend who does not like music, or your sister who wants to use it.

3. Describe a play you recently saw to your drama teacher, your parents, or a younger sibling.

### FOLLOW-UP
Focus discussion on the audience goal chosen. Why is the goal appropriate to the particular audience? How do the information and organization relate to the audience goal?

### ASSESSMENT
Assess each student's audience goal as he or she presents a speech to the class during this unit.

### ENRICHMENT
Have students role-play the situations.

# Chapter 10
## Finding and Using Information

This chapter focuses on teaching students to gather information for public speeches. Methods of research, such as library research, interviews, and surveys, are explained. Types of supporting material are also discussed. Criteria for analyzing evidence are presented. In Chapter 10 students will learn to:

- Explain a variety of ways to find information.
- Obtain information through an interview or survey.
- List various types of print materials used for research.
- Record research information properly.
- Describe various types of supporting material and list four kinds.
- Explain the difference between fact and opinion.

### WARM-UP ACTIVITIES

1. Have students list speech topics and as many ideas for sources as they can. List these on the board. Discuss with students the variety of sources available.

2. Ask students to bring an advertisement to class. Ask each student to identify which information in the advertisement is fact and which is opinion.

3. Ask students to describe how they usually gather information (library research, personal experience, and so on) for class assignments or in their daily life. Ask them what kinds of information (example, statistics, description, and so on) they use most often.

# CRITICAL THINKING ACTIVITIES

## Variety of Sources

### OBJECTIVE
To explain a variety of ways to find information

### MATERIALS NEEDED
Speech Source Sheet ❏

### PROCEDURE
Have students choose a speech topic and speech purpose. Then have them complete the Speech Source Sheet for that topic and purpose. Depending on the topic and purpose, students can choose to either interview an individual or conduct a survey. ❏

### FOLLOW-UP
Ask students to share their ideas in small groups. Such sharing can spark ideas.

### ASSESSMENT
Have students had in their Speech Source Sheets. Evaluate them for completeness and accuracy. ❏

### ENRICHMENT
Have students hand in a Speech Source Sheet for each speech they present.

# Speech Interest Inventory

### OBJECTIVE
To understand the importance of students looking at their own experiences for speech topics

### MATERIALS NEEDED
Speech Interest Inventory form ❑

### PROCEDURE
Ask each student to complete the Speech Interest Inventory form. ❑

### FOLLOW-UP
Have students share their inventories in small groups.

### ASSESSMENT
Collect the Speech Interest Inventories. Comment appropriately.

### ENRICHMENT
Students should keep these Inventories in their journals. Have them look at the Inventories when it is time to choose a speech topic. It is also a good idea to ask students to read through their Inventories from time to time to update their suggestions.

# Investigating Careers

## OBJECTIVE
To obtain information through interview research

## MATERIALS NEEDED
Interview Evaluation form ❑

## PROCEDURE
Divide the class into groups of five or six students. Assign each group a different career-related question to research. Ask each group member to interview a person in that career. After the interview, have the group members discuss what they found and select the most interesting information to present in class. The presentation may come in any form— TV or radio program, film, pictures, slides, magazine, or newspaper article.

Students could be directed to find out the following information:

1. What kind of training is necessary to become a spiritual leader in a particular religion (for example, to become a minister, rabbi, or mullah)?
2. What are the seasonal trends in flower and plant sales?
3. What training does a mechanic need to get started in a career?
4. What are advantages and disadvantages of different savings plans?
5. What do guidance counselors do?
6. How does someone become a school principal?
7. How does someone get into broadcast or print journalism?

## FOLLOW-UP
Ask students about the assignment:

1. What methods did you use to get information from your source (for example, asking direct questions, soliciting brochures, observing firsthand, etc.)? Which of these yielded the most information?
2. How did you select the information you would present?
3. If you were to do the assignment again, what would you do differently? Why?

## ASSESSMENT
Ask the person interviewed to complete and return the Interview Evaluation form. Have students complete analyses as well. ❑

## ENRICHMENT
Have students use interview research in at least one of their speeches during this unit.

# Let's Talk

### OBJECTIVE
To conduct an effective interview

### MATERIALS NEEDED
Variety of short fiction or biographies

### PROCEDURE
Have students work in pairs to read a book and then write a TV talk show script, in which one student acts as the host and interviews the other, who acts as one of the book's main characters. Students should take turns role-playing the host and book characters.

### FOLLOW-UP
Students should prepare a list of questions, practice asking follow-up questions, listen carefully and take notes if necessary, restate what was said and summarize when necessary, and end the interview by thanking the character.

### ASSESSMENT
Students can be assessed on their scripts and their performances. Did the host begin and end the interview gracefully? Were the host's questions interesting? Did the interviewee respond to the questions as the character might have responded?

### ENRICHMENT
Videotape the interviews and show them to the class.

# Oral History

## OBJECTIVE

To demonstrate competence in verbal, nonverbal, and listening skills by participating in interviews for the purpose of imparting information to an audience

## PROCEDURE

This assignment includes several steps. Students should begin by selecting a period of history or a specific event of importance to their communities that interests them. The only requirement is that the events have received enough attention so that they can be researched. The events selected can range from local floods to a small town's victory in the state basketball tournament.

Students should then select individuals who have had firsthand experience with the topics they have selected. Each student should interview one person.

Next, students should research the period or event they have selected. This research will culminate in a focused list of five to ten primary questions they intend to ask their interviewees. The students should make appointments of approximately one-half hour to interview the people they have selected. Interviews should be audiotaped.

After completion of their interviews, students should write papers critiquing their own performances. The self-evaluation paper should be divided into four segments:

1. Introductions that describe the topic area and explain why the particular interviewees were selected.

2. One- or two-page summaries of the research the student conducted before the interviews. This segment should also include a list of the primary questions the student planned to ask and should explain how the questions related to the research.

3. A transcript of a five-minute segment of the interviews that the student finds especially interesting.

4. An analysis of the transcript. Have the student evaluate the appropriateness of the primary questions, the quality of the follow-up questions, his or her ability to maintain control of the interview, the adequacy of his or her preparation, and any other concepts that have been stressed in class.

## Follow-Up

Ask students to describe the results of their interviews to the other class members. These descriptions may include both interesting facts that were obtained and information on what students feel were their strengths and weaknesses during the interviews.

## Assessment

Assess the introduction and research segments of the papers to identify any potential difficulties students may have had going into their interviews. Review the transcript segments to identify any major problems with student performances. Make sure the transcripts are composed in a clear and honest manner. Evaluation is weighted heavily toward the student's ability to thoroughly and accurately analyze his or her own performance using the concepts covered in class.

## Enrichment

Publish segments of the students' oral histories in the school newspaper or a class publication.

# Survey Savvy

### OBJECTIVE
To obtain information through the survey

### MATERIALS NEEDED
Journal Evaluation forms ❏

### PROCEDURE
Have students choose a speech topic that requires them to conduct an opinion poll. Sample topics might include "What do you think of the school cafeteria meals?" or "Should the drinking age be lowered to 16?" Instruct students to construct a survey relating to their topics and to analyze the results of the survey.

### FOLLOW-UP
Have students use the results of their surveys in future classroom speeches.

### ASSESSMENT
Evaluate the survey using one of the Journal Evaluation forms. ❏

### ENRICHMENT
Ask students to include their surveys in their journals and summarize their findings.

# Library Search

## OBJECTIVE
To list various types of print materials used for research[1]

## MATERIALS NEEDED
Questions for hunt

## PROCEDURE
Divide the class into small groups and send them on a library treasure hunt. Make up questions such as: What is the call number for *The Rise of the Computer State* by David Burnham? What magazines published articles on sharks last year? When did these articles appear? Who wrote *Pride and Prejudice?* Creating such a hunt forces students to become familiar with the library.

Treasure hunt questions can be divided by sources where answers may be found. Below are more ideas for sources and questions.

*Dictionaries and Encyclopedias*

1. Where did the phrase *ugly duckling* originate?

2. What was the original meaning of the word *flivver?*

3. How did Grandma Moses become famous?

4. Find a description of a moat.

5. What is existentialism?

*Almanacs, Yearbooks, and Atlases*

1. Through what states does U.S. Highway 1 run?

2. Who is the mayor of San Francisco?

3. Who won the World Series last year?

4. What are the major land uses in South America?

*Biographical References*

1. Which novel of Jessamyn West's became a popular movie?

2. What is the setting of John Steinbeck's novel *Of Mice and Men?*

3. Where can you find a picture of Tennessee Williams?

4. What novels did Upton Sinclair write?

### FOLLOW-UP

Have students share their answers. Help them become more familiar with the library by asking the school librarian to explain to them various resources.

### ASSESSMENT

Assessment of this activity is long-term. Students' research cards and bibliographies written later in the course will enable you to assess their use of the library.

### ENRICHMENT

You might have students create treasure hunts for each other. Or you can make this a competitive exercise among small groups to see who can find the most correct answers in the least amount of time.

# Research Cards

## OBJECTIVE

To record research information properly

## MATERIALS NEEDED

3 × 5 index cards (10 for each student)

## PROCEDURE

Instruct each student to prepare ten research cards for a speech topic of his or her choice. Cards should follow the format discussed in the text. In addition, all bibliographical references should be complete and entered correctly on the research card.

## ASSESSMENT

Have students hand in cards. Evaluate whether students used correct format for the cards and bibliographical entries.

## ENRICHMENT

For all speeches they present, have students hand in their research cards for you to evaluate.

# The Evidence Speaks for Itself

### OBJECTIVE
To describe and evaluate various types of supporting material

### MATERIALS NEEDED
3 × 5 index cards (6 for each student)

### PROCEDURE
Have students choose speech topics and purposes. Ask them to prepare six index cards for the topic—one representing each of the following: quotation, statistics, description, example, comparison/contrast, and personal experience.

### FOLLOW-UP
Ask students to write papers in which they analyze each piece of evidence according to the criteria discussed in the text.

### ASSESSMENT
Assess the research cards for completeness. Assess the journal writing according to how well each student was able to use the criteria in evaluating evidence.

### ENRICHMENT
Ask students to choose newspaper editorials and analyze the types of supporting material the author uses. Students can report their findings orally or write papers to include in their journals.

# Fact Versus Opinion

## OBJECTIVE
Describe the difference between fact and opinion

## PROCEDURE
Read the following story to students.[2] Then read the statements. Students should mark their answers *True, False,* or *?* (information not in story). Answers are given in parentheses.

> The only car parked in front of 619 Oak Street is a black one. The words "James M. Curley, M.D." are spelled in small gold letters across the left front door of that car.

*Statements about the story*

1. The color of the car parked in front      T    F    ?
   of 619 Oak Street is black.
   (The statement is definitely corroborated
   by information in the story.)

2. There are no words spelled across the left      T    F    ?
   front door of the car parked in front of 619
   Oak Street. (The statement is definitely
   contradicted by information in the story.)

3. Someone is ill at 619 Oak Street.      T    F    ?
   (Perhaps, but might the doctor live there?) .

4. The black car parked in front of 619 Oak      T    F    ?
   Street belongs to James M. Curley.
   (Could the car have been sold, leased, repossessed?)

Remind students to answer *only* on the basis of the information presented in the story. They must refrain from answering as they think it *might* have happened.

## FOLLOW-UP
Focus discussion on the difficulty caused when people confuse fact with opinion and vice versa.

## ASSESSMENT
On an objective exam, include a story like the one used in this activity. Ask students to mark statements about the story as fact or opinion.

## ENRICHMENT
Have students create their own stories and statements and share them with classmates.

# Notes

1. Adapted from Teacher's Edition for *Person to Person*.
2. The test is a section of *The Uncritical Inference Test*. Copies of the full-length test may be obtained from William V. Haney Associates, 2453 Cardinal Lane, Wilmette, IL 60091.

# Chapter 11
# Constructing the Speech

Organizing a speech is often difficult for students. This chapter focuses on the major organizational patterns and their relationships to speech topics and purpose sentences. Outlining is discussed. Stylistic elements such as memorable language and figures of speech are presented. Suggestions for creating effective introductions and conclusions are included. In Chapter 11 students will learn to:

- Describe five major organizational patterns for speeches.
- Identify the two major steps to organizing a speech.
- Decide which pattern works best for certain topics.
- Define a purpose sentence and give an example.
- Develop transitions to connect main ideas.
- Create full-sentence, phrase, or key-word outlines.
- Outline a speech using letters and numbers.
- List characteristics of language that gets the meaning across.
- Identify and give examples of figures of speech.
- Create introductions and conclusions that interest the audience.

## WARM-UP ACTIVITY

Scrambled Outline[1]

Write the following lists on the board. Have students organize them into an outline for the body of a speech. Have them start by finding the main points and then decide which subpoints develop the main points. The central idea of the speech is to inform the audience about major activities open to students in a high school.

| | |
|---|---|
| pamphlets | books |
| class work | wrestling team |
| extracurricular activities | parties |
| plays | baseball team |
| social events | term papers and speeches |
| tests | tennis club |
| periodicals | lectures |
| artistic events | athletic events |
| track team | swimming club |
| art exhibits | class discussion |
| dances | library research |
| learning activities | basketball team |

Have students share their completed outlines. Ask them the following questions. Where did differences occur? Why might they have occurred? Why is outlining important?

# CRITICAL THINKING ACTIVITIES

## Get Organized

### OBJECTIVE

To describe five major organizational patterns and decide which pattern works best for certain topics

### MATERIALS NEEDED

Organizational Pattern Analysis form ❏

### PROCEDURE

Present the five major organizational patterns to the class. Conduct a class discussion on how one topic (grading procedures) could be organized according to each pattern.

### FOLLOW-UP

Have each student choose a speech topic and write a short paper discussing how that topic could be organized by three of the five speech patterns. Students should include these papers in their journals.

### ASSESSMENT

Use one of the Journal Evaluation forms to assess the journal assignment. ❏

### ENRICHMENT

Use the Organizational Pattern Analysis form. ❏

# Examining Transitions

### OBJECTIVE
To develop transitions to connect main ideas[2]

### MATERIALS NEEDED
Recording of well-known speech

### PROCEDURE
Play a recording of a well-known speech, either from real life or from literature. Have students list all the transitional words or phrases the speaker uses and all the points at which they felt the speaker should have used a transition. Then read the speech to the class, omitting all the transitional words and phrases. Have the class tell you what parts of the speech they found confusing.

### FOLLOW-UP
Discuss the importance of transitions. Have students list as many transitional words and phrases as they can. Make a copy of the compiled list for each student.

### ASSESSMENT
Evaluate students' use of transitions as they present public speeches during this unit.

### ENRICHMENT
Ask students to evaluate the transitions that are used by their classmates during the speeches in this unit.

# A Sense of Purpose

## OBJECTIVE

To define a purpose sentence and give an example[3]

## PROCEDURE

Have students analyze the following purpose sentences. Which ones serve all of the functions of a purpose sentence? Have them rewrite the ones that do not.

1. Humans are wildlife's worst enemy.

2. Boating is an invigorating summer activity, but it can be dangerous unless one knows basic rules of boating safety.

3. There are many things one can do to keep a car looking good and running well for years.

4. Nearly every major U.S. city maintains a zoo, yet there is increasing evidence that most animals are not meant to be confined.

5. School standards are dropping.

6. There are several reasons everyone should jog: it's free, it's a great cardiovascular exercise, and it's known to improve mental health.

## FOLLOW-UP

Have students write a purpose statement for a speech topic of their choice.

## ASSESSMENT

Evaluate the purpose statement. On an objective exam, ask students to evaluate four or five different purpose statements.

## ENRICHMENT

Have each student create four purpose statements. Have students work with partners to critique one another's purpose statements.

# Outlining

### OBJECTIVE
To outline a speech using a key-word, phrase, or full-sentence outline

### MATERIALS NEEDED
Speech Preparation form ❑

### PROCEDURE
Assign students the preparation of a speech outline. They will use a topic of their choice and do research for the speech before presenting it. Have each student complete the Speech Preparation form. (Assign them this form for each speech they present.) Assign an outline using key words, phrases, or full sentences. Ask students to use all forms of outlining by the end of the public speaking unit. ❑

### FOLLOW-UP
Have students present their speeches.

### ASSESSMENT
Evaluate the speeches using one of the evaluation forms in Unit IV, Section A. Have students include their Speech Preparation forms in their journals. Evaluate these, paying particular attention to the outlines. ❑

### ENRICHMENT
Have students practice outlining.

# Memorable Language

## OBJECTIVE
To use language that gets the meaning across

## PROCEDURE
Write the following phrases on the board:

- parakeet in a cage
- moonlight on a beach
- traffic jam
- playing tennis in 90-degree weather
- one-year-old baby eating

Using these phrases, ask students to write memorable sentences by using language that is appropriate (assume the audience is this class), clear, accurate, and original (use figures of speech discussed in the text).

## FOLLOW-UP
Have students share their sentences. For each sentence created from the phrase, have the class vote on the most memorable description. Have students explain their reasons for choosing the sentence. Ask students to identify the various figures of speech included in the sentences.

## ASSESSMENT
Assess students' use of memorable language as they present their public speeches during this unit.

## ENRICHMENT
Have students include in their journals examples of memorable language they hear in daily conversation.

# Figuratively Speaking

## OBJECTIVE
To identify and give examples of figures of speech

## MATERIALS NEEDED
Selections of literature

## PROCEDURE
Choose a literary selection, either prose or poetry. In small groups, have students read the selection and identify the figures of speech.

## FOLLOW-UP
Have students discuss the examples they found. Then ask them to write figures of speech for the following: a sunny day, a little sister (brother), school, and happiness.

## ASSESSMENT
Evaluate students' use of figures of speech as they present public speeches during this unit.

## ENRICHMENT
Ask students to keep track of the figures of speech they hear people use during the next week. Have them include these in their journals.

# Beginnings and Endings

## OBJECTIVE
To create interesting introductions and conclusions

## PROCEDURE
Have students select topics for speeches. Have them list several ways to introduce the topic. Ask them to write three introductions using three methods. Using the same topic, have students list several ways to conclude a speech. Then have them write three conclusions using three methods.

## FOLLOW-UP
Ask volunteers to read their introductions to the class. Let students indicate which introduction is most effective and why. Ask volunteers to read their conclusions to the class. Let class members indicate which conclusion is most effective and why. Some questions for students to consider:

1. After hearing the introduction, do you want to hear the rest of the speech? Do you know what the speaker's audience goal is? Did you recognize the purpose statement? Do you have a general idea of what will be covered in the speech?

2. After hearing the conclusion, what do you feel about the topic? Is the conclusion effective in summarizing the purpose and audience goal?

## ASSESSMENT
Evaluate students' introductions and conclusions as they present public speeches during this unit.

## ENRICHMENT
Ask students to evaluate three of their classmates' speech introductions and conclusions during this unit. Have them include their evaluations in their journals.

## Notes

1. Adapted from *Person to Person* Teacher's Resource Book.
2. "CCISD Resource Materials for Speaking and Listening in the Secondary Reading Program." Corpus Christi Independent School District, Corpus Christi, TX, 1985, p. 22.
3. Adapted from *Person to Person* Teacher's Resource Book.

# Chapter 12
# Delivering the Speech

Students often fear public-speaking experiences. This chapter begins by discussing stage fright and ways to develop speech confidence. Rehearsal techniques that help build speech confidence are included. The major focus of this chapter is on delivery, both vocal characteristics and nonverbal characteristics. The chapter concludes by discussing the use and misuse of visual aids. In Chapter 12 students will learn to:

- Define *stage fright* and describe ways of developing speech confidence.

- Describe the four methods of delivery and explain when each might be used.

- List the nonverbal factors in delivery and explain their importance.

- Explain how to rehearse a speech.

- Describe guidelines for making and using audiovisual aids.

## WARM-UP ACTIVITIES

1. Discuss why most performers—actors, athletes, public speakers—are nervous before a performance. Have students discuss what they do when they are nervous and how these nervous habits can be eliminated or lessened.

2. Play videotapes of various speakers. Ask students to discuss the delivery characteristics they thought were effective and those they thought were ineffective.

3. Students who are athletes might discuss how they mentally prepare for a game or event.

# CRITICAL THINKING ACTIVITIES

## Stage Fright

### OBJECTIVE

To define *stage fright* and describe ways of developing speech confidence

### PROCEDURE

Have each student interview someone who often speaks in public to find out what they do to minimize stage fright.

### FOLLOW-UP

After completing the interviews, instruct students to write a one-page paper summarizing what they learned. The paper should be included in their journals. Then suggest that students discuss their findings with one another in small groups. Focus the discussion on ways to increase speech confidence as discussed in the text.

### ASSESSMENT

Assess the journal assignment using one of the Journal Evaluation forms.
❏

### ENRICHMENT

Have students write papers in their journals describing how their stage fright lessened during this unit.

# Nonverbal Delivery

### OBJECTIVE
To list nonverbal factors in delivery (initial impression, vocal characteristics, movement, facial expressions, and gestures) and explain their importance[1]

### PROCEDURE
The way a speaker walks to the podium creates an initial impression. Invent ten to twenty characters and have students walk to the podium as those characters. Among the characters you might include: a student who is about to receive the school medal for excellence in math; a person who is being honored for setting up a shelter for abandoned pets; a principal about to give bad news to the school board; an Olympic medal winner at a press conference; an Olympic medal winner unjustly accused of taking a stimulant to increase performance. You may want to have students speak one sentence as these characters. In any case, discuss the nonverbal behavior of the characters—their walks, posture, facial expressions, and gestures.

### FOLLOW-UP
To illustrate that nonverbal cues are numerous and vital to effective communication, let ten students each take a turn speaking with hands behind their backs. Don't let them practice. The time limit for these speeches should be two minutes or less. Suggested topics for handless impromptu speeches include: how to make a set shot in basketball; how to mix a cake; how to clean fingernails; how to wash your face; or how to serve a tennis ball. Then let the same ten students give the same speeches using their hands. The time limit should be one minute. Then discuss the differences between the two speeches.

### ASSESSMENT
Ask students how they felt when they listened to speeches without seeing hand gestures. Did they think that meaning was lost, that the speaker was hindered, or that the speaker didn't mind? Ask them if their bodies and muscles tensed while watching their "handless" classmates. Then ask the speakers how they felt.

### ENRICHMENT
Videotape the speeches. View each student's performance with him or her individually. Discuss with each student ways to improve nonverbal delivery.

# Rehearsal Session

## OBJECTIVE
To explain how to rehearse a speech

## MATERIALS NEEDED
Journal Evaluation form ❏

## PROCEDURE
Copy the following Rehearsal Session chart on the board. Ask each student to complete it for one of their assigned speeches. Based on the results, ask students to write papers considering what they did in their sessions that was helpful and what they did that wasn't.

| Time | Place | # of minutes practiced | What you did during the practice session |
|------|-------|------------------------|------------------------------------------|
|      |       |                        |                                          |

## FOLLOW-UP
In class, have students share the results of their journal assignment. Then have the class generate a list of things to do during rehearsal sessions.

## ASSESSMENT
Assess the journal assignment using one of the Journal Evaluation forms. ❏

## ENRICHMENT
Have students complete the Rehearsal Sessions journal assignment for each speech they give.

# Effective Visual Aids

## OBJECTIVE
To describe guidelines for making and using visual aids

## MATERIALS NEEDED
A variety of visual aids
Visual Aid Evaluation form ❏

## PROCEDURE
Present six to ten visual aids one at a time. (Save some from each of your classes. Some should be very good and some not so good.) Ask students to identify specific criteria that make the visual aids acceptable or unacceptable.

## FOLLOW-UP
Ask students to describe visual aids they have seen speakers use. Did the speakers follow the guidelines for making and using visual aids?

## ASSESSMENT
Assess students' ability to identify and apply the criteria for effective visual aids.

## ENRICHMENT
Have each student choose a speech topic that lends itself to the use of a visual aid. Have students present their speeches for the class, using a visual aid. Ask classmates to evaluate each student's speech using the Visual Aid Evaluation form. ❏

# Vocal Critique

## OBJECTIVE
To demonstrate effective use of voice and diction in presenting speeches

## MATERIALS NEEDED
A Caldecott or Newbery Medal–winning book ❑
Vocal Critique Sheet ❑

## PROCEDURE
Have students read one of the Caldecott or Newbery award winners listed in Unit IV, Section A. Each student should write a one- to two-minute speech to persuade other students to read the chosen book. Each speech should be audiotaped and played for the class. ❑

## FOLLOW-UP
After each speech is played, have students complete the Vocal Critique Sheet and discuss the strengths and weaknesses of the vocal delivery. They should also discuss how the use of voice and diction affected their reaction to the speech. ❑

## ASSESSMENT
Using the Vocal Critique Sheet, evaluate each audiotape. ❑

## ENRICHMENT
Have students create a radio show. If you like, you can audiotape the show and play it for other classes.

# Impromptu Box

## OBJECTIVE
To generate impromptu speech topics and present impromptu speeches

## MATERIALS NEEDED
Small box or container
Impromptu Speech Evaluation form ❑

## PROCEDURE
Obtain a small box or container and place it in a conspicuous place in the classroom. Tell students that the box is set aside for impromptu speaking topics. Ask students to be on the lookout for interesting information that would be challenging to talk about for one or two minutes. The kinds of things that students should contribute to the box might be brief, humorous stories, factual trivia from newspapers and magazines, interesting statistics from record books, and whatever else may catch their fancy. Contributions should be made on 3 x 5 index cards. Each student should check the topic with you before putting it in the box.

## FOLLOW-UP
Periodically ask students to go to the box, draw a topic, and make a one- or two-minute impromptu speech on the topic they select.

## ASSESSMENT
Use the Impromptu Speech Evaluation form to assess the impromptu speeches. ❑

## ENRICHMENT
The more often students are asked to speak impromptu, the easier it will be for them. As students feel more comfortable with this type of speaking, increase the time limit of the speeches.

# I Wrote It Myself

## OBJECTIVE
To write a manuscript for a speech or memorized presentation

## PROCEDURE
Have students write informative or persuasive speeches. Make sure all students write the same type of speech. Discuss with students the most important aspects of the type you've asked them to write. The importance of a good outline prior to writing the speech in manuscript form should be stressed, as well as transitions, effective introductions, conclusions, and organizational patterns.

## FOLLOW-UP
Have students share their speeches with one another. Based on peer feedback, students may revise their speeches prior to handing them in for grading.

## ASSESSMENT
Evaluate the written manuscripts. When students perform the speeches, the oral delivery should also be evaluated.

## ENRICHMENT
Present the speeches to another class or to an all-school assembly.

# Speech Models

## OBJECTIVE
To analyze and evaluate written speech models

## MATERIALS NEEDED
Printed speeches from *Vital Speeches,* speech anthologies, or student speeches

## PROCEDURE
Provide model speeches for students. Ask each student to read his or her assigned speech and be ready to discuss the following:

1. Type of speech

2. Main points

3. An outline of the speech

4. Examples of evidence used

5. Stylistic devices

6. Effective writing

## FOLLOW-UP
Focus the class discussion on the above six items. Have students provide reasons for their answers.

## ASSESSMENT
Give an examination in which students are provided a different model speech and are required to discuss in writing the six points listed in the procedure section.

## ENRICHMENT
Have students write short informative speeches. In pairs or small groups, have them critique one another's written speeches.

# Note

1. From *Person to Person Teacher's Resource Book.*

# Chapter 13
## Creating the Informative Speech

Students are often called upon to present informative speeches. This chapter presents the most common type of informative speeches students will be asked to give. Evaluation of informative speeches is also discussed. In Chapter 13 students will learn to:

- List principles for making a speech memorable.
- Create an informative speech.
- Create a number of social ritual speeches.
- Define *constructive criticism.*
- List guidelines for constructive criticism.
- Critique a speech to inform.

## WARM-UP ACTIVITIES

1. Ask students to present one- to two-minute impromptu speeches. (You may wish to use the Impromptu Speech Topics and Impromptu Speech Evaluation forms.) ❏

2. Ask students to list the number of informative speeches they have heard in the last week. List these on the board. Discuss the importance of informative speaking in everyday life.

# CRITICAL THINKING ACTIVITIES

## Memorable Communication

### OBJECTIVE
To list principles for making a speech memorable

### MATERIALS NEEDED
Magazines with advertisements
Tapes of TV and radio commercials

### PROCEDURE
Have each student bring in at least one magazine advertisement. Ask students to analyze the advertisement in terms of the principles for making a speech memorable. Then tape some television or radio commercials. Play the tapes for students. Ask them to analyze the commercials in terms of the principles for making a speech memorable.

### FOLLOW-UP
Ask each student to write his or her own memorable advertisement for a favorite movie or book, or for a fictitious product.

### ASSESSMENT
Evaluate the student-produced advertisements according to their effectiveness in using the principles.

### ENRICHMENT
Have students prepare commercials for their favorite books or movies, or for fictitious products. Videotape the commercials. Have the class vote on the most memorable commercial. What elements made it so memorable?

# Information, Please

## OBJECTIVE
To create an informative speech

## MATERIALS NEEDED
Informative Speech Evaluation form ❑
Speaker's Speech Evaluation form ❑

## PROCEDURE
As a final project, have students prepare a six- to eight-minute informative speech. Assign a student to critique each speech.

## FOLLOW-UP
Have students present the speeches in class.

## ASSESSMENT
Evaluate the speeches using the Informative Speech Evaluation form. Students should also evaluate their own speeches and write a paper analyzing their performance using the Speaker's Self-Evaluation form. ❑

## ENRICHMENT
Videotape each student's speech. Discuss with each student individually his or her strengths and weaknesses.

# I Know What the Judge Will Say

## OBJECTIVE
To evaluate information given by others[1]

## MATERIALS NEEDED
Videotape of "People's Court"
"People's Court" Viewing Sheet ❏
"I Know What the Judge Will Say" Evaluation form ❏

## PROCEDURE
Watch a segment of "The People's Court" on videotape, stopping just before the judge is about to return with his decision. Break students into groups of five to six and share perceptions of what the judge's decision will or should be. Appoint one student in each group to serve as observer/evaluator, using the "I Know What the Judge Will Say" Evaluation form.

Each small group should present to the class its decision concerning the ruling. Then, as a class, watch the judge's decision on the television monitor. Evaluate the decision of the judge and of the small groups and watch the segment again from the beginning. ❏

## FOLLOW-UP
Students should reevaluate their decisions after hearing the final ruling. They should examine whether they were considering all the important factors and then come to a class decision. Have each group observer/evaluator report on small-group procedures in his or her group and share information reported on the evaluation form.

## ASSESSMENT
Observe the small groups as they work. Complete an "I Know What the Judge Will Say" Evaluation form for each group. ❏

## ENRICHMENT
Using the "People's Court" Viewing Sheet, have students discuss what information they gained from nonverbal communication. ❏

# Announcing . . .

## OBJECTIVE
To create a number of social ritual speeches

## MATERIALS NEEDED
Social Ritual Speech Evaluation form ❏

## PROCEDURE
Arrange to have students take turns giving the announcements for each school day over the public address system. Students should be responsible for making sure each announcement contains the necessary information for the day on which they are to give the announcements.

## FOLLOW-UP
Discuss with students the importance of vocal characteristics when speaking over a public address system. Why is it important for the speaker to pay particular attention to rate, volume, and clarity?

## ASSESSMENT
Have students evaluate each announcer's performance by using the Social Ritual Speech Evaluation form. Rather than a written critique, have students give their comments orally. ❏

## ENRICHMENT
During the course of the school year, arrange to have your students nominate a candidate at a school assembly, present awards at school assemblies or parent-teacher meetings, and welcome audiences to school assemblies. Evaluate by using the Social Ritual Speech Evaluation form. ❏

# Responding to Rituals

## OBJECTIVE

To demonstrate awareness of standards for public ritual by reporting responses to public speeches or ceremonies

## MATERIALS NEEDED

Role Play Evaluation form ❑

## PROCEDURE

Have students observe public rituals such as a sermon, a commencement speech, a political speech, a meeting of the city government or state legislature, a wedding, a graduation, a baptism, or a bar mitzvah.

## FOLLOW-UP

Have students write one-page reactions to the events they observed. The reaction should describe the event, the rituals within it, and why the rituals were important to the event's success.

## ASSESSMENT

Have students share their observations in small groups. Collect their one-page reactions.

## ENRICHMENT

Students might like to role-play some of the rituals. Evaluate the role play using the Role Play Evaluation form. ❑

# Constructive Criticism

## OBJECTIVE
To list and utilize guidelines for constructive criticism

## PROCEDURE
Have students prepare three-minute informative speeches on how to do something. Have them choose one of the following topics or one of their own.

- How to make potato salad
- How to eat a pomegranate
- How to warm up before jogging
- How to keep your Boston fern (or other plant) alive
- How to hook up new speakers to your old receiver
- How to replace the plug on an electric appliance
- How to throw a curveball
- How to get a part-time job
- How to operate a videocassette recorder
- How to give a large dog a bath

## FOLLOW-UP
Have students present their speeches to the class and assign students to evaluate each speech. The critiques should be given orally. Other class members should list the critic's use of the guidelines for constructive criticism. Following the speeches and critiques, focus class discussion on which guidelines were used and which were not.

## ASSESSMENT
Evaluate each critic's use of the guidelines.

## ENRICHMENT
Throughout the public-speaking unit, ask students in their critiques to use the guidelines for constructive criticism.

# Group Critique

### OBJECTIVE
To critique a speech to inform[2]

### PROCEDURE
Have students prepare informative speeches and practice them in small groups before giving them for the entire class. Tell the small groups that they are to coach the speakers, providing feedback to help improve the speech before it is given to the class.

### FOLLOW-UP
Have students present the speeches in class.

### ASSESSMENT
Ask each student to write a one-page analysis of how he or she changed the speech as a result of the small group's feedback. Students should include their papers in their journals. Evaluate the papers as a part of the journal grading.

### ENRICHMENT
If possible, repeat this activity periodically during this unit.

## Notes

1. Adapted from *Classroom Activities in Listening and Speaking*, pp. 41, 64, 70.
2. From *Person to Person Teacher's Resource Book*.

# Chapter 14
## Creating the Persuasive Speech

Chapter 14 focuses on persuasive speaking and distinguishes it from informative speaking. Methods of organizing a persuasive speech are presented. Types of faulty reasoning, audience attitudes, and ways for students to make themselves believable are discussed. Types of reasoning are described. The process of evaluating persuasive speeches is explored. In Chapter 14 students will learn to:

- Define *persuasion* and *persuasive speaking.*

- Explain the difference between speaking to inform and speaking to persuade.

- List and describe Maslow's five human needs.

- Describe ways to make yourself believable.

- Identify various types of reasoning.

- Recognize examples of faulty reasoning.

- Create a speech according to the problem-solution outline.

- Evaluate a persuasive speech.

### WARM-UP ACTIVITIES
1. Play the "Millionaire" game in class. Tell the class that it has one million dollars to award to the most deserving cause. Each student will be given an opportunity to persuade the class that his or her cause should get the money.

2. Collect junk mail for several weeks. Bring it to class. Ask students to discuss what the sender is trying to persuade the receiver to do. What persuasive techniques are used? Are students persuaded? Why or why not?

3. Have students describe three arguments they would use to persuade a three-year-old to eat spinach. List the persuasive strategies on the board. Discuss with the class which arguments might be most effective.

4. Have each student give a speech on a subject about which he or she has strong feelings—something that arouses the student's indignation or anger. In giving vent to their feelings, students should make a real attempt to let go. Tell them to move freely about the speaking area, let their faces reflect their emotions, pound the lectern, and shake their fists. The object is for them to approach expressive action with abandon, and not worry about overdoing it.

# CRITICAL THINKING ACTIVITIES

## The Sixty-Second Commercial

### OBJECTIVE
To list and describe Maslow's five human needs

### PROCEDURE
Ask studens to work with partners to design a sixty-second commercial for a fictitious product. Encourage them to be creative. Have students present the commercials. Commercials must be in good taste and no longer than sixty seconds. Each must include a visual aid.

### FOLLOW-UP
After each commercial is presented, students should discuss which needs the commercial appealed to. The creator of the commercial should state which needs he or she intended to appeal to.

### ASSESSMENT
On an objective test, ask students to describe Maslow's five human needs. Evaluate how students appealed to various human needs during their speeches in this unit.

### ENRICHMENT
Ask students to analyze how they use appeals to Maslow's human needs in their daily lives—when trying to persuade others, empathize with others, or inform others.

# Believability

## OBJECTIVE

To describe ways of achieving believability

## MATERIALS NEEDED

Speaker Believability form ❑

## PROCEDURE

Have students come to class with persuasive speaking topics. They should also come to class with the Speaker Believability form completed. ❑

## FOLLOW-UP

Have students work in pairs to share their Believability forms. Ask each partner to state whether he or she finds the persuader believable. Change partners and repeat the activity three or four times.

## ASSESSMENT

In their journals, have students write an analysis of this activity answering the question "What did I learn about my believability as a persuader?"

## ENRICHMENT

At the end of this unit, have students write a short journal entry analyzing whether their believability has improved during this unit and why.

# I Believe . . .

## OBJECTIVE
To express feelings via a public speech on a topic of personal interest or concern

## MATERIALS NEEDED
Personal Interest Speech Evaluation form ❑

## PROCEDURE
Have students choose a topic of interest or concern to them. Each student should present a two- to three-minute speech in which at least three feelings are expressed. For example, a student might speak on how she or he feels about cheating and why.

## FOLLOW-UP
After all speeches are presented, the class discussion should focus on how students felt about expressing their feelings. Was it difficult? Why or why not?

## ASSESSMENT
Evaluate speeches using the Personal Interest Speech Evaluation form. ❑

## ENRICHMENT
Have students evaluate one another's speeches using the Personal Interest Speech Evaluation form. ❑

# With Good Reason

## OBJECTIVE
To identify various types of reasoning

## PROCEDURE
Have each student speak for two minutes on one of the following topics:

- My allowance should be raised.
- My curfew should be extended.
- I should have been an only child.

Each speech should contain three reasons. The audience should take note of the type of reasoning used by the speaker.

## FOLLOW-UP
List on the board the four types of reasoning discussed in the text. Ask students to list examples of each type of reasoning from the speeches. Decide if the examples meet the criteria for good reasoning.

## ASSESSMENT
On an objective exam, ask students to identify the type of reasoning in various statements. Ask them to describe whether the reasoning is sound.

## ENRICHMENT
In their journals, students should examine and analyze the reasoning used in an editorial from a newspaper or newsmagazine.

# Faulty Reasoning

## Objective
To recognize examples of faulty reasoning

## Procedure
Ask students to keep track of examples of faulty reasoning they hear during the week. These can be from friends, parents, teachers, or the media. They should try to list examples of all the kinds listed in the text.

## Follow-Up
Have students share examples from their lists, explaining why the reasoning is faulty.

## Assessment
On an objective test, ask students to identify types of faulty reasoning. Watch for faulty reasoning contained in student speeches given during this unit.

## Enrichment
Ask students to repeat this assignment later in the unit.

# Persuasive Speech Critique

### OBJECTIVE
To evaluate a persuasive speech

### MATERIALS NEEDED
Persuasive Speech Critique Sheet ❑
Persuasive Speech Evaluation form ❑

### PROCEDURE
Have each student listen to a persuasive speech on the radio or television, or in their community.

### FOLLOW-UP
Ask students to write papers in which they (1) describe the organizational pattern, (2) discuss how the speaker made herself or himself believable, and (3) discuss any faulty reasoning they heard. Students should also complete the Persuasive Speech Critique Sheet. ❑

### ASSESSMENT
Evaluate the assignment using the Persuasive Speech Evaluation form. ❑

### ENRICHMENT
Have students write letters to the speaker suggesting how he or she could improve the speech. Letters should be saved in students' journals.

# Let Me Persuade You

## OBJECTIVE
To create a speech according to the problem-solution format

## MATERIALS NEEDED
Speech evaluation form ❏

## PROCEDURE
Ask each student to prepare a six- to eight-minute persuasive speech using the problem-solution format. Assign a student to critique each speech.

## FOLLOW-UP
Have each student present his or her speech and critique a classmate's speech.

## ASSESSMENT
Evaluate speeches using one of the evaluation forms in Unit IV, Section A. ❏

## ENRICHMENT
Have students present their speeches to real audiences such as the Rotary Club, school board, or other community groups.

# Chapter 15
## Learning About Debate

This chapter presents a basic introduction to debate. Debate propositions, how debate works, and values of debate are covered. In Chapter 15 students will learn to:

- Define *debate, rebuttal,* and *refutation.*
- Distinguish between the affirmative and negative side.
- Describe the values of debate.
- Explain three types of debate propositions.
- Create a workable proposition.
- Define ways you can create arguments.
- Describe two debate formats.

### WARM-UP ACTIVITIES
1. Invite a lawyer or judge to class to talk to students about courtroom debate.
2. Show the film *Mr. Smith Goes to Washington.* Discuss the debate strategies that appeared in the film.
3. Ask students to think about the debates they have in their everyday lives—with parents, teachers, siblings, or friends. Use their examples to show them how important debate skills can be.

# CRITICAL THINKING
# ACTIVITIES

## Propositions

### OBJECTIVE
To create a workable proposition and to differentiate between the three types of debate propositions[1]

### PROCEDURE
Have students identify the flaw in each of the following propositions and explain which characteristic of a good proposition is missing. Then have students identify each proposition as to type (fact, policy, or value).

Resolved: That the military draft should be reinstated with registration at local high schools.

Resolved: That the federal government should establish comprehensive security guidelines for United States airports to make them safe.

Resolved: That the federal government should increase social welfare programs in the current budget.

Resolved: That city government should establish a program to better enforce the collection of parking fines.

Resolved: That enrollment in elementary schools is rising.

Resolved: That fresh vegetable prices fluctuate with the growing seasons.

Resolved: That the federal government should redesign the tax structure to tax citizens equally and use a significant portion of the tax dollars to improve the educational system.

Resolved: That the federal government should establish a comprehensive program to provide medical care for all Americans.

## Follow-Up

Have students rewrite the propositions correctly. Have them write three propositions they would be interested in debating. The propositions can involve school policy, local policy, state regulations, or federal issues. Have them take one of the propositions and explain how it meets the characteristics of a good proposition.

## Assessment

Have students write propositions that meet all the criteria for good propositions and label the propositions as to type.

## Enrichment

Ask the class to choose one of the propositions. Each student should create a two- to three-minute affirmative argument and a two- to three-minute negative argument. Students should then present their arguments orally. Arguments should be evaluated according to (1) evidence and reasoning used, (2) organization, and (3) delivery.

# Refutation and Rebuttal

## OBJECTIVE
To create arguments in refutation and rebuttal speeches[2]

## PROCEDURE
Organize some mini debates, in which students are assigned to present one fully developed argument of no more than three minutes in length. The class listens and takes notes, is given five minutes to think of arguments, and then several members are asked to give rebuttal speeches. Following this, the entire class critiques the activity.

## FOLLOW-UP
The student giving the argument can refute the other students' rebuttal speeches. Other students may then give suggestions for ways they would have refuted the rebuttal arguments. Ask students to discuss how refutation and rebuttal help build a case.

## ASSESSMENT
Have students analyze their own performances and include the analysis in their journals. Students should ask themselves:

1. Did I present my arguments clearly?

2. Did I support my arguments with evidence?

3. Was my delivery effective?

## ENRICHMENT
Students can choose a proposition and repeat the activity. They should analyze their performance and write a paper comparing their performance to the previous one, noting any improvements and listing areas still needing improvement.

# The Value of Debate

## OBJECTIVE
To describe the values of debate

## MATERIALS NEEDED
Journal Evaluation form ❑

## PROCEDURE
Students should be asked to think about their activities during this unit and to then briefly state how participation in debate has helped them enhance their (1) research skills, (2) organizational skills, (3) critical thinking and listening skills, and (4) speaking skills. The statements should be included in their journals.

## ASSESSMENT
Evaluate the journal assignment using one of the Journal Evaluation forms. ❑

## ENRICHMENT
Students might write short editorials on the value of debate for their school newspaper.

# Notes

1. Adapted from Lynn Goodnight, *Getting Started in Debate* (Lincolnwood, IL: National Textbook Co., 1993).

2. Adapted from Maridell Fryar, David A. Thomas, and Lynn Goodnight, *Teacher's Guide to Basic Debate* (Lincolnwood, IL: National Textbook Co., 1989).

# Part Five
# Interpretive Communication

Too often students confuse oral interpretation with acting. In their introduction to *Oral Interpretation in the Secondary School*, Herman and Ratliffe make the distinction very clear:

> There is a distinct difference between oral interpretation and acting. Acting is indirect because drama usually assumes a "fourth wall" so that the actor seldom has personal contact with the audience. Furthermore, drama is limited to the scene, those characters, and those specific costumes. In interpretative reading, the imaginative appeal gives the audience a warehouse of all the sets in the world, characters limited only by the imagination of the listener and the skill of the reader, and a motivation to interpret an experience with more variation than the best movies can provide. (p. x)

You might discuss the idea of the "fourth wall" and how it has no place in oral interpretation. Students need to understand that personal contact with the audience is important; that communication is accomplished only when there's a relationship between the performers, audience, and literature.

Performing literature can contribute significantly to students' personal growth. Current writers claim that performing literature helps students improve their thinking skills and develop a sense of good literature. Students also learn communication skills, because the emphasis in oral interpretation and group interpretation is on group cooperation and social awareness.

We suggest that teachers make evaluation criteria very clear to students at the outset of this unit. Critiquing and evaluating oral interpretation performances can be difficult. The clearer the criteria, the easier this task will be.

# Chapter 16
# Preparing for Oral Interpretation

This chapter is a basic introduction to oral interpretation. It discusses criteria for selecting literature and describes ways to identify and analyze the important elements of literature such as dramatic speaker, word choice, and style. In Chapter 16 students will learn to:

- Define *oral interpretation.*

- List various sources of material for oral interpretation.

- Describe the standards for selecting literature.

- Select quality literature for performance.

- Describe the four keys to analyzing literature for performance.

## WARM-UP ACTIVITIES

1. Have each student make a list of his or her favorite books. (You may wish to have students complete the Reading Interest Inventory form in Unit IV, Section A of the *Resource Book.*) Share the lists. Which books are familiar to most students? Which ones would students like to hear read? ❑

2. Invite a local radio or television personality to discuss the role of oral interpretation in radio and television performance.

3. Hold a class discussion on the topic "What examples of oral interpretation can be found in everyday life?"

4. Ask each student to bring to class a favorite piece of literature. In small groups have students discuss why they chose these selections. Pair students to read each other's selections. Then have them discuss whether the selection is good literature, using the criteria for good literature discussed in the text.

# CRITICAL THINKING ACTIVITIES

## Oral Interpretation Resource File

### OBJECTIVE
To list sources and develop a file of oral interpretation material

### MATERIALS NEEDED
Folders and a small expandable file for each student

### PROCEDURE
Instruct students to look for material for oral interpretation. Students will label separate files according to the following categories: favorite authors, anthologies, biographies and autobiographies, movies and plays, oral history, and personal and friends' writings.

### FOLLOW-UP
During one class period, class members may share their files with each other.

### ASSESSMENT
Collect the files and evaluate them in terms of completeness and literary quality of the selections.

### ENRICHMENT
Create a class file. Each student should choose her or his favorite selection to contribute.

# Family Oral History

## OBJECTIVE
To collect oral histories from students' families

## MATERIALS NEEDED
Coat of Arms sheet ❑

## PROCEDURE
Develop a Favorite Family Story sheet with the following categories—story, person telling story, something about storyteller. Have students ask some relatives to tell them interesting or funny family stories and use the Favorite Family Story sheet to write down their favorites, along with something about the person(s) who told the stories.

## FOLLOW-UP
Have each student make a family coat of arms and share it with classmates. These coats of arms could be displayed in the classroom. ❑

## ASSESSMENT
Students should include the oral histories in their journals. The family coats of arms could be evaluated for originality.

## ENRICHMENT
Have students perform their oral histories.

# Choosing Literature for Performance

## OBJECTIVE
To describe and use standards for selecting quality literature

## MATERIALS NEEDED
Oral Interpretation Evaluation form ❑

## PROCEDURE
Have students choose a piece of literature and plan a performance for a group of small children, classmates, or parents. Have students consider the criteria for choosing literature discussed in the text. Ask them to pay particular attention to selecting literature appropriate to each of the audiences and deciding how they would change the presentation for each audience. Have them write their analyses and include these in their journals. Students could also discuss their analyses in small groups.

## FOLLOW-UP
Have students role-play the various audiences while other students perform their selections. Focus discussion on what general techniques are appropriate for each audience and whether student performers used these techniques for their specific audiences.

## ASSESSMENT
Evaluate performances using one of the Oral Interpretation Evaluation forms. ❑

## ENRICHMENT
Perform the selections for the three types of audiences.

# Analyzing Literature

### OBJECTIVE
To describe the four keys to analyzing literature for performance

### MATERIALS NEEDED
Literature Analysis form ❏

### PROCEDURE
Ask students to bring to class selections from literature they would like to perform. Have each student complete the Literature Analysis form. ❏

### FOLLOW-UP
Meet with each student to discuss the Literature Analysis forms or have students work in pairs to discuss them. ❏

### ASSESSMENT
Evaluate the Literature Analysis forms on accuracy and completeness. ❏

### ENRICHMENT
Have students perform the prose for an audience other than their class-mates. For example, you might invite parents to an Oral Interpretation Night and have students perform their prose selections for their parents.

# Chapter 17
# Performing Oral Interpretation

This chapter focuses on preparing a script for performance. Several rehearsal techniques are discussed. The roles of eye focus, gestures, facial expressions, and voice in the performance of oral interpretation are emphasized. Also included are criteria for evaluating oral interpretation performances. In Chapter 17 students will learn to:

- Prepare a script for oral interpretation.

- Write an introduction to your literature.

- Establish eye focus to support the literature.

- Use vocal variety, gestures, and facial expressions to create mood and characters.

- Mark a script for performance.

- Use a variety of rehearsal techniques.

- Evaluate an oral interpretation performance.

## WARM-UP ACTIVITIES
1. Poetry readings set to music are highly successful. Have each student select a favorite poem. The music will provide the background for an oral reading. You will be surprised and pleased to see how beautifully student readers perform as they respond to the musical background. Students may bring in recordings. They may also provide live music for each other's readings.

2. Using the statement "Yes, I will ask her," have students communicate the following meanings through voice variation:

    - Of course, I'll ask her.

    - I'm really not going to ask her.

    - Who said I would ask her?

    - I'll ask her, will you?

    - I don't know if I'll ask her.

    - For the tenth time, I'll ask her.

    - Yes, I'll ask her, but I don't want to.

Discuss how different meanings are created through differences in volume, rate, pause, and eye focus.

# CRITICAL THINKING ACTIVITIES

## Preparing a Script

### OBJECTIVE
To prepare a script for oral interpretation

### MATERIALS NEEDED
Journal Evaluation form ❑
Selections suitable for oral interpretation

### PROCEDURE
Preparing a script will include several steps—cutting the script, arranging the material, and organizing the script. You may give students class time to do these steps.

### FOLLOW-UP
Have students write in their journals about their experience in preparing a script. Scripts can also be used with the Practice Makes Perfect activity later in this section.

### ASSESSMENT
As students work in class, evaluate their progress in preparing the script. Evaluate their journals using one of the Journal Evaluation forms. ❑

### ENRICHMENT
Ask students to keep journals of how they performed each step, what they found to be most helpful and effective in their approach to each step, and what advice they would give other students preparing a script for oral interpretation.

# To Cut or Not to Cut

## OBJECTIVE

To understand what elements can be cut from a selection; to prepare a cutting of a selection

## PROCEDURE

During class time, have students write in their own words a well-known fairy tale. Then have students read their fairy tale versions to the rest of the class.

## FOLLOW-UP

Discuss the idea of cutting a selection. Compare the various cuttings of the fairy tale, focusing on where different students chose to begin and end their tale, how and what variations on a known story were manifest, what was left out of certain tales and why that might be so; assuming some students begin "Once upon a time . . .," discuss the text and order of the fairy tale, conventions of forms, acceptance of conventions, and how this relates to plot, theme, and mood.

Have students bring in the selections they've chosen for performance and prepare cuttings.

## ASSESSMENT

On a written exam, give students a section of a short story to cut. Have them explain why they cut the story as they did. Evaluate the cutting they choose based on criteria for classroom performance.

## ENRICHMENT

Students can share their cuttings with classmates—either in small groups or in pairs. Does the cutting make sense to the others in the group?

# Introducing Oral Interpretation

## OBJECTIVE
To write an introduction to an oral interpretation selection

## MATERIALS NEEDED
Introduction Evaluation form ❑

## PROCEDURE
Ask students to choose any of the selections included at the end of the text chapter and write an introduction.

## FOLLOW-UP
Have students present their introductions to the class. Ask classmates if, based on the introduction, they want to hear the selection.

## ASSESSMENT
Use the Introduction Evaluation form to evaluate the introductions. ❑

## ENRICHMENT
After students have written their introductions, but prior to performing them, have them share their introductions in small groups and revise based on classmates' suggestions.

# My Voice Says It All

## OBJECTIVE
To use vocal variety to create mood and characters

## PROCEDURE
Have students do any of the following activities:

1. Play a game of moods. Communicate anger, sorrow, joy, excitement, surprise, fear, and shyness while saying, "And then our eyes met." Vary by using other sentences and feelings.

2. Play the emphasis game. Use any sentence and emphasize a different word each time you say it. For example, "I am going home." Discuss the variety of meanings communicated by placing the emphasis on different words.

3. Read a passage using different rates and pauses. Discuss the effect on a listener. Also note what pauses can do to change meaning. For example, "When are you coming for dinner?"

4. To practice various vocal qualities, select a story with dialogue spoken by a variety of characters. How can the reader make the characters appear to be different? What would happen if Papa Bear's words were read with a tiny voice? How would a "proud emperor with new clothes" speak?

5. Have fun with words by saying them with different inflections, volume, rate, and pitch. Tell or make up jokes, riddles, and limericks that rely on vocal qualities for effectiveness.

6. Practice reading to appropriate musical accompaniment to help effective vocal quality. For example, use marching band music for patriotic literature and lyrical music for spring, elves, and fairies. Using this technique, try reading Walter de la Mare's "Silver," Carl Sandburg's "Jazz Fantasia," Vachel Lindsay's "The Congo," or Elinor Wylie's "Sea Lullaby."

7. Say the alphabet to create impressions of anger, sadness, happiness, surprise, frustration.

## FOLLOW-UP
Tape-record oral interpretation selections as they are read aloud. Encourage each student to listen to his or her reading and suggest improvements that could be made in vocal variety.

## ASSESSMENT
Have students include a self-analysis of their vocal variety in their journals.

## ENRICHMENT

Ask students to tape-record one or more of these exercises periodically during this unit and write papers analyzing their vocal improvement.

# Pantomime Impromptu

## OBJECTIVE
To use gestures, eye focus, and facial expressions to create mood and character

## PROCEDURE
Ask students to pantomime simple actions, for example, sewing on a button, ironing a shirt, putting on makeup, shaving, cracking an egg into a bowl, building a snowman, casting a line.

## FOLLOW-UP
Have each student prepare a pantomime of her or his choosing that tells a story. For example, a student might pantomime getting ready for a first date. The pantomime should use eye focus, facial expressions, and gestures to create mood and characterization. Classmates should guess (1) the situation, (2) the mood, and (3) the type of character.

## ASSESSMENT
Evaluate the effectiveness of each student's gestures and facial expressions in creating mood and characters as he or she performs oral interpretations during this unit.

## ENRICHMENT
Based on classmates' feedback, have students perform their pantomimes again. Comment on improvement.

# Folktales

### OBJECTIVE
To use verbal and nonverbal skills to tell a folktale

### MATERIALS NEEDED
Storytelling Evaluation forms ❑

### PROCEDURE
Ask students to recall their favorite folktales. Discuss why they liked them (fast-moving plot, suspense, easily identifiable characters). Tell each student to prepare a folktale to tell.

### FOLLOW-UP
Have students tell their folktales.

### ASSESSMENT
Evaluate storytelling using one of the Storytelling Evaluation forms. ❑

### ENRICHMENT
Have students create modern fairy tales or tell folktales from different character's perspectives. For example, tell "The Three Little Pigs" from the wolf's perspective. (You might read to the class *The True Story of the Three Little Pigs* by Jon Scieska [New York: Scholastic, 1989].) Ask students to form a storytelling troupe and perform for elementary school children.

# Practice Makes Perfect

## OBJECTIVE
To use a variety of rehearsal techniques

## MATERIALS NEEDED
The students' prepared scripts from the earlier activity, Preparing a Script

## PROCEDURE
After students have prepared their selections, review with them the rehearsal techniques discussed in the text. Then give them the following directions: Ask a partner to listen to you as you practice. This classmate should note whether you are using enough eye contact with your audience. He or she should also point out any mannerisms that may distract the audience from your efforts to convey your author's ideas and emotions. Write your partner's suggestions on your reading copy, then conduct a practice session alone.

## FOLLOW-UP
Have students present their selections to their partners again and discuss the improvements.

## ASSESSMENT
Evaluate each student's final performance of the selection using one of the critique sheets in Unit IV, Section A. ❑

## ENRICHMENT
Have students tape-record their practice sessions to find out whether they are emphasizing the sections they intended to and whether they are building effectively to the climax of their selection.

# These Marks Mean Something

## OBJECTIVE
To mark a script for oral interpretation

## MATERIALS NEEDED
Selections suitable for oral interpretation

## PROCEDURE
Have students choose any of the selections included in the text chapter and mark the selection they have chosen.

## FOLLOW-UP
Working with partners, have students exchange their marked scripts and evaluate them for clarity and emphasis.

## ASSESSMENT
Discuss with each student his or her markings.

## ENRICHMENT
In small groups, have students read their marked scripts to one another and critique the effectiveness of each other's marking systems.

# I'll Be the Critic

## OBJECTIVE
To establish criteria and use it to critique an oral interpretation performance

## MATERIALS NEEDED
Oral Interpretation Evaluation forms ❑

## PROCEDURE
Student critics can be assigned each day to give oral critiques. Thoughtful evaluations are more likely to be obtained if only two or three students are assigned to fill out the forms rather than each member of the class. You might assign speaker numbers and put these in triplicate into a box. Ask each student to draw three numbers for an evaluation assignment.

## FOLLOW-UP
Using one of the Oral Interpretation Evaluation forms, have students critique classmates' performances. ❑

## ASSESSMENT
Have students hand in their critique forms. Look for accuracy and completeness.

## ENRICHMENT
Based on their critiques of classmates' performances, ask students to write papers analyzing the best performance or on the topic, "What Makes an Oral Interpretation Performance Effective?"

# Group Storytelling

### OBJECTIVE
To learn to tell a story

### MATERIALS NEEDED
Four short fables (for example, four from Arnold Lobel's award-winning book, *Fables* [New York: Harper and Row, 1980])
Storytelling Evaluation forms ❑

### PROCEDURE
Divide students into groups of four. Assign each group a fable. Have students read the fables silently. Have the groups discuss their initial impressions of the fables. Then have them read aloud, with each member having a turn to read. Ask students to discuss what they learned about the story after they read it aloud. Have them read the story aloud again, with each student reading a different passage from the one he or she read before. Have group members discuss: If you were a picture book artist, which moments of the story would you choose to illustrate? Why? Describe the illustrations in detail.

Have students turn the text over and try a group telling, taking turns just as they did when they were reading. After the groups have finished, have them look back at the text and discuss what was left out and what additions were made that brought the story to life. (Most groups discover at this point that it is a good idea to memorize Lobel's morals just as he phrased them. This will be the only memorized part of the story; the rest will flow naturally from the students' knowledge of the story.) Have students try a second group telling. Have them stand up for this telling.

Finally, have each student literally "tell the story to the wall." Each student should move to the wall and tell the story. This time is used for a dress rehearsal of the telling. Recombine the students into new groups of four so no teller is with a member of his or her previous group. Each group member now tells his or her fable. Have students share with one another the strengths of each student's telling.

### ASSESSMENT
Group members could evaluate one another's stories using one of the Storytelling Evaluation forms. ❑

### ENRICHMENT
Have students present their stories for another class.

# Chapter 18
# Group Interpretation

This chapter defines *group interpretation* and describes ways to perform choral reading and readers' theatre. It also focuses on evaluating these oral performances. In Chapter 18 students will learn to:

- Define *group interpretation, choral speaking,* and *readers' theatre.*

- List criteria for selecting material for choral speaking and readers' theatre.

- Describe a variety of group performance techniques.

- Prepare and perform a choral speaking selection.

- Prepare and perform a readers' theatre presentation.

- Evaluate group interpretation performances.

## WARM-UP ACTIVITIES

1. Have students read "Echo for Three Voices" in Unit IV, Section A of the *Resource Book.* Assign parts and have students read the parts aloud. ❏

2. Choose a poem you particularly like (or use one included in the text). Have students read the poem as a choral reading.

# CRITICAL THINKING
# ACTIVITIES

## Selections for Choral Speaking

### OBJECTIVE
To list criteria for selecting material for choral speaking[1]

### PROCEDURE
Ask students to bring in poems they feel are appropriate for choral reading. Using the criteria in the text, ask them to explain why the pieces are appropriate.

### FOLLOW-UP
Focus class discussion on determining why the selections are appropriate.

### ASSESSMENT
Evaluate the appropriateness of the material students chose by using the criteria discussed in the text.

### ENRICHMENT
Help students create an original script for choral reading. Focus on a single familiar activity, such as a slumber party, stage fright, or baby-sitting. Brainstorm with the class for specific words and phrases that capture their feelings and recreate the event. Record these words and phrases on the board and begin to shape them into clusters or poetic fragments. Read through the tentative script together, arranging, adding, and subtracting details, before settling on a final version. Designate, with student advice, individual and group parts and begin rehearsal. The final readings can be presented to other classes, at assembly programs, and at parent-teacher meetings.

# Choral Speaking Techniques

## OBJECTIVE
Describe techniques for performing choral reading

## PROCEDURE
Using one of the pieces included at the end of the text chapter, discuss with students performance-technique options to use when performing the piece for choral speaking.

## FOLLOW-UP
Try out students' suggestions for techniques. Discuss which ones worked best and why.

## ASSESSMENT
Based on class discussion, assess the students' understanding of, and ability to use, the techniques discussed in the text.

## ENRICHMENT
As a journal assignment, have students choose a piece of literature and discuss possible performance technique options for a choral speaking performance of the literature.

# Choral Speaking Evaluation

## OBJECTIVE
To evaluate choral speaking performances

## MATERIALS NEEDED
Choral Speaking Self-Evaluation form ❏
Choral Speaking Evaluation form ❏

## PROCEDURE
Have students complete the Choral Speaking Self-Evaluation form and include it in their journals. ❏

## FOLLOW-UP
In small groups, have students share their self-evaluations with others. ❏

## ASSESSMENT
Evaluate the Self-Evaluation forms as part of each student's journal. ❏

## ENRICHMENT
Throughout this unit, students should also evaluate the choral speaking performances of their classmates and include the Choral Speaking Evaluation forms in their journals. At the end of the choral speaking unit, have students write a one-page paper in which they discuss the general strengths and weaknesses of the classroom performances. ❏

# All Together Now

## OBJECTIVE
To prepare and perform a choral reading

## MATERIALS NEEDED
Choral Speaking Evaluation form ❑

## PROCEDURE
Working in committees, have students select and prepare a choral reading presentation of poems for younger children. This may be built around a theme, such as "Lions, Tigers, and Bears, Oh My!"; "School Days"; "Seasons of the Year"; or "Who's Afraid of the Big Bad Wolf?"

## FOLLOW-UP
Share the performance with young children.

## ASSESSMENT
Assess the script using the criteria discussed in the text. Assess the performance using the Choral Speaking Evaluation form. ❑

## ENRICHMENT
Organize a "tour" for the students. Have them perform the choral reading presentation to several audiences of children.

# Literature for Reader's Theatre

## OBJECTIVE
To select material appropriate for reader's theatre

## MATERIALS NEEDED
Selections appropriate for reader's theatre

## PROCEDURE
Ask each student to bring in a piece of literature he or she feels is appropriate for reader's theatre. Using the criteria listed in the text, ask for explanations of why the material is appropriate.

## FOLLOW-UP
Focus class discussion on determining why the selections are appropriate.

## ASSESSMENT
Evaluate the appropriateness of the material students chose.

## ENRICHMENT
Have students work in groups. Have each group choose a theme and write an original reader's theatre script. The scripts could be performed for other classes.

# Preparing for Reader's Theatre

### OBJECTIVE

To describe techniques for performing reader's theatre

### PROCEDURE

Using one of the selections at the end of the chapter, discuss with students the performance-technique options for performing reader's theatre.

### FOLLOW-UP

Try out students' suggestions. Discuss which ones worked best and why.

### ASSESSMENT

Based on class discussion, assess the students' understanding of, and ability to use, the techniques discussed in the text.

### ENRICHMENT

As a journal assignment, have students choose a piece of literature and discuss possible performance-technique options for the reader's theatre performance of the literature.

# Reader's Theatre Performance

## OBJECTIVE
To prepare and perform reader's theatre

## MATERIALS NEEDED
Reader's Theatre Evaluation forms ❏

## PROCEDURE
As a final project for this unit, have students create a multimedia reader's theatre program in which they use at least one medium other than the literature. For example, they may use slides projected behind the readers, music, or sound effects. Have students perform the reader's theatre.

## ASSESSMENT
Evaluate using one of the Reader's Theatre Evaluation forms. ❏

## ENRICHMENT
Compile a children's program using reader's theatre. Take it to various grade schools or Sunday schools, or present it on Saturday at the children's section of your local library. Scripts could be developed from authors such as Rudyard Kipling, Beatrix Potter, Dr. Seuss, A. A. Milne, Mercer Mayer, or Maurice Sendak. Also, books such as *Charlotte's Web,* by E. B. White, or *Alexander & the Terrible, Horrible, No Good, Very Bad Day,* by Judith Viorst, lend themselves to reader's theatre.

# Evaluating Reader's Theatre

### OBJECTIVE

To evaluate reader's theatre performances

### MATERIALS NEEDED

Reader's Theatre Evaluation forms ❏

### PROCEDURE

Using one of the Reader's Theatre Evaluation forms, have students evaluate the reader's theatre performances of their classmates, and include these in their journals. ❏

### ASSESSMENT

Evaluate the critiques as a part of each student's journal.

### ENRICHMENT

Ask students to write a two- to three-page paper in which they pull together the evaluations they have completed and write a general critique of the class's performances.

## Note

1. From "Resource Materials for Speaking and Listening in the Secondary Language Arts Program."

# UNIT III

# RESOURCES

## Resources for Professional Growth

### Print

Books and articles on teaching speech communication

Allen, R. R., Kenneth Brown, and Joanne Yatvin. *Learning Language Through Communication: A Functional Approach*. Belmont, CA: Wadsworth, 1986.

Allen, R. R., S. Clay Willmington, and Jo Sprague. *Communication in the Secondary School: A Pedagogy*. 3rd ed. Scottsdale, AZ: Gorsuch Scarisbrick, 1990.

Barker, Larry, ed. *Communication in the Classroom*. Englewood Cliffs, NJ: Prentice-Hall, 1982.

Bassett, Ronald, and Mary Boone. "Improving Speech Communication Skills: An Overview of the Literature." In Rebecca Rubin, ed. *Improving Speaking and Listening Skills*. San Francisco: Jossey, Bass, 1983, pp. 83–93.

Bock, Douglas G., and E. Hope Bock. *Evaluating Classroom Speaking*. Urbana, IL: ERIC and Speech Communication Association, 1981.

Boileau, Don. "Speaking/Listening; Much Used, Little Taught." *NASSP Curriculum Report.* Reston, VA: National Association of Secondary School Principals, 14 (December 1984).

Book, Cassandra, and Kathleen Galvin. *Instruction in and about Small Group Discussion.* Urbana, IL: ERIC and Speech Communication Association, 1975.

Callahan, Joseph, and Leonard Clark. *Teaching in the Middle and Secondary Schools: Planning for Competence.* New York: Macmillan, 1982.

Civikly, Jean. *Classroom Communication.* Dubuque, IA: William C. Brown, 1992.

*Classroom Activities in Speaking and Listening.* Madison, WI: Wisconsin Department of Public Instruction, 1991.

Cooper, Pamela J., ed. *Activities for Teaching Speaking and Listening in Grades 7–12.* Annandale, VA: Speech Communication Association, 1985.

Cooper, Pamela J. *Speech Communication for the Classroom Teacher.* 4th ed. Scottsdale, AZ: Gorsuch Scarisbrick, 1991.

Cooper, Pamela J., and Kathleen Galvin. *Improving Classroom Communication.* Washington, DC: Dingle Associates, 1982.

Friedman, Paul. *Communicating in Conferences: Parent-Teacher-Student Interaction.* Urbana, IL: ERIC and Speech Communication Association, 1980.

Friedrich, Gustav, ed. *Education in the 80's: Speech Communication.* Washington, DC: National Education Association, 1981.

Gallo, Donald R. *Books for You.* Urbana, IL: National Council of Teachers of English, 1985.

Galvin, Kathleen, and Bernard Brommel. *Family Communication: Cohesion and Change.* 3rd ed. New York: Harper Collins, 1991.

Gudykunst, William, and Young Yun Kim. *Communicating with Strangers: An Approach to Intercultural Communication.* 2d ed. New York: McGraw-Hill, 1992.

*Guidelines for Developing Oral Communication Curricula in Kindergarten Through Twelfth Grade,* 1991. Available from the Speech Communication Association, 5105 Backlick Rd., Bldg. #E, Annandale, VA 22003.

Hawley, Robert C., and Isabel Hawley. *Human Values in the Classroom: A Handbook for Teachers.* New York: Hart, 1975.

Hays, Ellis R. *Interact: Communication Activities for Personal Life Strategies.* San Francisco: International Society for General Semantics, 1974.

Hetherington, M. Sue. "The Importance of Oral Communication." *College English,* 44 (October 1982): 570–574.

Holbrook, Hilary Taylor. "Oral Language: A Neglected Language Art?" *Language Arts,* 60 (February 1983): 255–258.

Jensen, J. Vernon. "Oral Skills Enhance Learning." *Improving College and University Teaching*, 28 (Spring 1980): 78–80.

Johnson, Eric. *Teaching School: Points Picked Up*. New York: Walker and Co., 1981.

Klopf, Donald W. *Intercultural Encounters: The Fundamentals of Intercultural Communication*. Englewood, CO: Morton, 1987.

Larson, Carl E. "Problems in Assessing Functional Communication." *Communication Education*, 27 (November 1978): 304–309.

Littlejohn, S. *Theories of Human Communication*. 4th ed. Belmont, CA: Wadsworth, 1992.

Lounsbury, John H. "As I See It: The Most Neglected (and Important?) Basic." *Middle School Journal*, XV (August 1984): 2.

Lukens, Rebecca. *A Critical Handbook of Children's Literature*. Glenview, IL: Scott, Foresman, 1986.

May, Frank B. *To Help Children Communicate*. Columbus, OH: Charles Merrill, 1980.

Newmann, Dara. *The New Teacher's Almanack*. West Nyack, NY: Center for Applied Research in Education, 1980.

Pfeiffer, J. William, and John E. Jones, eds. *A Handbook of Structured Experiences for Human Relations Training*. 8 vols. Iowa City, IA, and La Jolla, CA: University Press Associates, 1973–1983.

Probst, Robert. *Adolescent Literature: Response and Analysis*. Columbus, OH: Charles Merrill, 1984.

Reed, Anthea J. S. *Reaching Adolescents: The Young Adult Book and the School*. New York: CBS College Publishing, 1985.

Rubin, Don, and Nancy Mead. *Large Scale Assessment of Oral Communication Skills K–12*. Urbana, IL: ERIC, 1984.

Samovar, Larry, and Richard Porter. *Intercultural Communication*. 6th ed. Belmont, CA: Wadsworth, 1991.

Seiler, William, L. David Schuelke, and Barbara Lieb-Brilhart. *Communication for the Contemporary Classroom*. New York: Holt, Rinehart, and Winston, 1984.

Sharan, Shlomo, and Yael Sharan. *Small Group Teaching*. Englewood Cliffs, NJ: Educational Technology Publications, 1976.

Simon, Sidney B., Leland W. Howe, and Howard Kirschenbaum. *Values Clarification: A Handbook for Teachers and Students*. New York: Hart, 1972.

*Speech Communication Teacher*. A quarterly journal of speech activities available from the Speech Communication Association Convention, 5105 Backlick Road, Bldg. #E, Annandale, VA 22003.

Spolin, Viola. *Improvisation for the Theatre: A Handbook for Teaching and Directing Techniques*. Evanston, IL: Northwestern University Press, 1983.

Stewart, Lea, Alan Stewart, Sheryl Friedley, and Pamela Cooper. *Communication Between the Sexes*. 2d ed. Scottsdale, AZ: Gorsuch Scarisbrick, 1990.

Tannen, Deborah. *You Just Don't Understand: Women and Men in Conversation*. New York: Ballantine, 1990.

Tanner, F. A. *Basic Drama Projects*. Caldwell, ID: Clark Publishing Company, 1977.

Thaiss, Christopher, and Charles Suhor, eds. *Speaking and Writing K–12*. Urbana, IL: National Council of Teachers of English, 1984.

Wood, Barbara. *Children and Communication*. 2d ed. Englewood Cliffs, NJ: Prentice-Hall, 1981.

Wood, Barbara, ed. *Development of Functional Communication Skills: Grades 7–12*. Urbana, IL: ERIC and Speech Communication Association, 1977.

# Professional Associations

American Alliance for Theatre and Education, c/o Joan Lazarus, Lowell Hall, University of Wisconsin, Madison, WI 53706.

American Forensics Association, c/o James Pratt, University of Wisconsin–River Falls, River Falls, WI 54022.

American Speech and Hearing Association, 10801 Rockville Pike, Rockville, MD 20852.

Association for Theatre in Higher Education, c/o Gil Lozier, School of Theatre, Florida State University, Tallahassee, FL 32306.

International Communication Association, Balcones Research Center, 10100 Burnet Road, Austin, TX 78758.

International Listening Association, 366 North Prior Avenue, St. Paul, MN 55104.

National Association for the Preservation and Perpetuation of Storytelling, P.O. Box 309, Jonesborough, TN 37659.

National Catholic Forensics League, Jackson Avenue and Emory Road, Mineola, NY 11501.

National Council of Teachers of English, 1111 Kenyon Road, Urbana, IL 61801.

National Forensics League, Ripon, WI 54871.

Speech Communication Association, 5105 Backlick Road, Bldg. #E, Annandale, VA 22003.

# Teaching Aids for Speech

Write for Catalogs:

Audiotronics, 7428 Bellaire, North Hollywood, CA 91605.

Audio Visual Promotion Aids, 466 Lexington Avenue, New York, NY 10017.

Charles Beseler Company, 8 Fernwood Road, Florham Park, NJ 07932

Design Resources, Box 193, Williamstown, MA 01267.

Films for the Humanities, Box 2053, Princeton, NJ 08540.

G. & T. Harris, Inc., 215 Lexington Avenue, New York, NY 10016.

L. & M. Stagecraft, 2110 Superior Avenue, Cleveland, OH 44114.

Slide Presentations, Publishers, 175 Fifth Avenue, New York, NY 10010.

Speech Communication Association, 5105 Backlick Road, Bldg. #E, Annandale, VA 22003.

Visual Resources, Inc., 152 West 42nd Street, Suite 1219, New York, NY 10036.

# Part Resources

Following are additional resources for each part. The resources are divided into two sections, print resources and nonprint resources.

## Part One

### PRINT RESOURCES

Beyer, Edwin, Charlotte Lee, and Charles Wilkinson. *Speaking of: Communication, Interpretation, and Theatre.* Glenview, IL: Scott, Foresman, 1975.

Buys, William E., Thomas Sill, and Roy Beck. *Speaking by Doing: A Speaking-Listening Text.* 6th ed. Lincolnwood, IL: National Textbook Company, 1991.

Cooper, Pamela, ed. *Activities for Teaching Speaking and Listening: Grades 7–12.* Annandale, VA: Speech Communication Association, 1991.

Galvin, Kathleen. *Listening by Doing.* Lincolnwood, IL: National Textbook Company, 1988.

Galvin, Kathleen, and Cassandra Book. *Person to Person: An Introduction to Speech Communication.* 5th ed. Lincolnwood, IL: National Textbook Company, 1994.

Steil, Lyman. *The Secondary Teacher's Listening Resource Unit.* St. Paul, MN: Communication Development, Inc., 1982.

Wolvin, Andrew, and Carolyn Coakley. *Listening Instruction.* Urbana, IL: ERIC, 1979.

### NONPRINT RESOURCES

Barr Films, P.O. Box 5667, Pasadena, CA 91107. "You're Not Listening," 21 min., color film.

Centron Corporation, Box 687, 1621 W. 9th St., Lawrence, KS 66044. "Communication by Voice and Action," 2d ed., 14 min., 16mm color film. "Planning Your Speech Film," 13 min., 16mm color film. "Some Hear—Some Listen," 12 min., 16mm color film.

*Communication: Person to Person.* Contact Series I: Communications and the Media. Englewood Cliffs, NJ: Scholastic Book Services.

"Communication—the message." Chicago: Coronet Instructional Media, 1977.

"Communication—the receiver." Coronet Films, 65 East South Water Street, Chicago, IL 60601.

"Communication—the sender." Coronet Films, 65 East South Water Street, Chicago, IL 60601.

"Study Skills: How to Listen Effectively." Guidance Associates, 16mm., 1988.

# Part Two

## PRINT RESOURCES

Barbour, Alton, and Alvin A. Goldberg. *Interpersonal Communication: Teaching Strategies and Resources.* Urbana, IL: ERIC and Speech Communication Association, 1974.

Burgoon, Judee K., David B. Buller, and W. Gill Woodall. *Nonverbal Communication: The Unspoken Dialogue.* New York: Harper and Row, 1989.

Canfield, Jack, and Harold Wells. *100 Ways to Enhance Self-Concept in the Classroom: A Handbook for Teachers and Parents.* Englewood Cliffs, NJ: Prentice-Hall, 1976.

DeVito, Joseph A. *The Interpersonal Communication Book.* 5th ed. New York: Harper and Row, 1989.

DeVito, Joseph. *Messages: Building Interpersonal Relationships.* New York: Harper and Row, 1990.

Kelly, Marylin McGregor, and Joseph A. DeVito. *Experiences Activities Manual.* New York: Harper and Row, 1990.

Knapp, Mark, and Judith Hall. *Nonverbal Communication in Human Interaction.* 3rd ed. New York: Holt, Rinehart and Winston, 1992.

Pfeiffer, J. William, and Jane E. Jones, eds. *A Handbook of Structural Experiences for Human Relations Training.* 8 vols. Iowa City, IA, and La Jolla, CA: University Press Associates, 1973–1983.

Ratliffe, Sharon A., and Deldee M. Herman. *Self-Awareness: Communicating with Yourself and Others.* Lincolnwood, IL: National Textbook Company, 1989.

Stewart, John. *Bridges Not Walls.* 5th ed. New York: McGraw-Hill, 1990.

Trenholm, Sarah, and Arthur Jensen. *Interpersonal Communication.* 2d ed. Belmont, CA: Wadsworth, 1992.

Watson, Kittie W., and Larry L. Barker. *Interpersonal and Relational Communication.* Scottsdale, AZ: Gorsuch Scarisbrick, 1990.

Weaver, Richard L., II. *Understanding Interpersonal Communication.* 5th ed. Glenview, IL: Scott, Foresman/Little Brown, 1990.

## Nonprint Resources

"Am I Worthwhile?" Communications Park Video, Box 5000, Mt. Kisco, NY 10544.

"The Art of Two-way Communication." Dartnell, 4660 North Ravenswood Avenue, Chicago, IL 60640.

"Barriers to Communicating." Resources for Education and Management, Inc., 544 Medlock Road, Decatur, GA 30030.

CRM Films, 2233 Faraday Ave., Suite F, Carlsbad, CA 92008.

*Clear as Mud*, 10 min., color film.

"Communicating Non-Defensively: Don't Take It Personally," 21 min., color film.

"Communication! The Nonverbal Agenda," 21 min., color film.

"Perception," 28 min., color film.

"The Power of Listening," 26 min., color film.

"Productivity and the Self-Fulfilling Prophecy: The Pygmalion Effect," 27 min., color film.

"Verbal Communication: The Power of Words," 30 min., color film.

Michigan State University, Audiovisual Department, East Lansing, MI 48824. "Interpersonal Communication" videocassette, 22 min., color, beta or VHS.

# Part Three

## Print Resources

Barker, Larry L., Kathy J. Wahlers, Kittie W. Watson, and Robert J. Kibler. *Groups in Process: An Introduction to Small Group Communication.* 3rd ed. Englewood Cliffs, NJ: Prentice-Hall, 1987.

Book, Cassandra, and Kathleen Galvin. *Instruction in and about Small Group Discussion.* Urbana, IL: ERIC and Speech Communication Association, 1975.

Borisoff, Deborah, and David A. Victor. *Conflict Management: A Communication Skills Approach.* Englewood Cliffs, NJ: Prentice-Hall, 1989.

Brilhart, John K. *Effective Group Discussion.* 6th ed. Dubuque, IA: William C. Brown, 1989.

Johnson, David, and Frank Johnson. *Joining Together: Group Theory and Group Skills.* 3rd ed. Englewood Cliffs, NJ: Prentice-Hall, 1987.

Kell, Carl, and Paul Corts. *Fundamentals of Effective Group Communication.* New York: Macmillan, 1980.

Prentice, Diana, and James Payne. *More Than Talking: Analysis and Activities in Group Communication.* Caldwell, OH: Clark Publishing, 1983.

Robert, Henry M., III, and William J. Evans, eds. *Robert's Rules of Order.* Glenview, IL: Scott, Foresman, 1990.

Tiberius, Richard. *Small Group Teaching: A Trouble Shooting Guide.* Toronto, Canada: OISE Press, 1990.

Tubbs, Stewart. *A Systems Approach to Small Group Communication.* 4th ed. New York: McGraw-Hill, 1992.

## Nonprint Resources

Coronet Films. 65 East South Water Street, Chicago, IL 60601:

"Discussion in Democracy," film

"Parliamentary Procedure," film

"Parliamentary Procedures in Action," film

Coronet/MTI Film and Video, 1108 Wilmot Road, Deerfield, IL 60015:

"Aids to Speaking," 15 min., 16mm color film

"Destination: Communications" (part of the EPCOT Educational Media Collection), 20 min., 16mm color film

"Listen Well, Learn Well," 2d ed., 11 min., 16mm color film

"Planning Your Speech," 13 min., 16mm color film

"Stage Fright," 13 min., 16mm color film

CRM Films, 2233 Faraday Ave., Suite F, Carlsbad, CA 92008:

"Group Dynamics: Groupthink," 22 min., color film

"Leadership: Style or Circumstance," 28 min., color film

"Capitalizing on Group Dynamics." Resources for Education and Management, Inc., 544 Medlock Road, Decatur, GA 30030.

"Conducting a Meeting." McGraw-Hill, 1221 Avenue of the Americas, New York, NY 10036.

"Speech-Group Discussion." University of Michigan Audio Visual Center, 416 South Street, Ann Arbor, MI 48109.

Ban Films, Box 5667, Pasadena, CA 91107:

"You're Not Communicating"

"You're Not Listening"

# Part Four

## Print Resources

Bartanen, Michael, and David Frank. *Lincoln–Douglas Debate.* Lincolnwood, IL: National Textbook Company, 1994.

Beebe, Steven, and Susan Beebe. *Public Speaking: An Audience-Centered Approach.* Englewood Cliffs, NJ: Prentice-Hall, 1991.

Bock, Douglas, and E. Hope Bock. *Evaluating Classroom Speaking.* Urbana, IL: ERIC and Speech Communication Association, 1981.

Buys, William E., Thomas Sill, and Roy Beck. *Speaking by Doing.* 6th ed. Lincolnwood, IL: National Textbook Company, 1991.

Fryar, Maridell, David A. Thomas, and Lynn Goodnight. *Basic Debate.* 3rd ed. Lincolnwood, IL: National Textbook Company, 1989.

Goodnight, Lynn. *Getting Started in Debate.* 2d ed. Lincolnwood, IL: National Textbook Company, 1992.

Gronbeck, Bruce, Raymie McKerrow, Douglas Ehninga, and Alan Monroe. 11th ed. *Principles and Types of Speech Communication.* New York: HarperCollins, 1990.

HopKins, Mary F., and Beverly Whitaker, eds. *Contemporary Speech.* Lincolnwood, IL: National Textbook Company, 1982.

Ilardon, Joseph A. *Speaking Persuasively.* New York: Macmillan, 1981.

Littlejohn, Stephen W., and David M. Jabusch. *Persuasive Transactions.* Glenview, IL: Scott, Foresman, 1992.

Lucas, S. *The Art of Public Speaking.* 4th ed. New York: McGraw-Hill, 1992.

Misiewicz, Joe, and Mary Wise, eds. *Debate in the Secondary School.* Lincolnwood, IL: National Textbook Company, 1979.

Oddo, Linda, and Thomas McClain. *Student Congress.* Lincolnwood, IL: National Textbook Company, 1994.

Osborn, M., and S. Osborn. *Public Speaking.* 2d ed. Dallas: Houghton-Mifflin, 1991.

Prentice, D., and J. Payne. *Public Speaking Today.* Lincolnwood, IL: National Textbook Company, 1989.

Sitzman, M., and R. Garcia. *Successful Interviewing.* Lincolnwood, IL: National Textbook Company, 1981.

Sprague, Jo, and Douglas Stuart. *The Speaker's Handbook.* 3rd ed. Fort Worth, TX: Harcourt-Brace Jovanovich College Publishers, 1992.

Stewart, C. *Teaching Interviewing for Career Preparation.* Urbana, IL: ERIC and Speech Communication Association, 1991.

Thomas, David A., and John P. Hart, eds. *Advanced Debate.* 4th ed. Lincolnwood, IL: National Textbook Company, 1993.

Wood, Roy V., and Lynn Goodnight. *Strategic Debate.* 4th ed. Lincolnwood, IL: National Textbook Company, 1989.

Ziegelmueller, George, Jack Kay, and Charles Dause. *Argumentation: Inquiry and Advocacy.* 2d ed. Englewood Cliffs, NJ: Prentice-Hall, 1990.

## Nonprint Resources

"Speech: Planning Your Talk." McGraw-Hill/Young America Films, 1221 Avenue of the Americas, New York, NY 10036.

"Your First Speech." Bailey Films/BFA Educational Media, 2211 Michigan Avenue, Santa Monica, CA 90404.

"Using Visuals in Your Speech." McGraw-Hill, 1221 Avenue of the Americas, New York, NY 10036.

"Critical Thinking—Making Sure of the Facts." Coronet Films, 65 East South Water Street, Chicago, IL 60601.

"Delivering Your Speech." Resources for Education and Management, Inc., 544 Medlock Road, Decatur, GA 30030.

Michigan State University, Audiovisual Department, East Lansing, MI 48824. "Small Group Communication" videocassette, 24 min., color, beta or VHS.

"Speak Up: Skills of Oral Communication." The Center for Humanities Video, 60 minutes for all six parts. Two videotapes. Color, VHS, 1977 and 1986.

"Speaking Effectively: To One or One Thousand," 21 min., color film. CRM Films, 2233 Faraday Ave., Suite F, Carlsbad, CA 92008.

"How to Speak with Confidence." VHS, distributed by Nightingdale Conant Corporation, Chicago, 1987, 48 min.

# Part Five

## Print Resources

Cooper, Pamela, and Rives Collins. *Look What Happened to Frog: Storytelling in Education.* Scottsdale, AZ: Gorsuch Scarisbrick, 1992.

Heinig, Ruth Beall, and Lyda Stillwell. *Creative Dramatics for the Classroom Teacher.* 3rd ed. Englewood Cliffs, NJ: Prentice-Hall, 1988.

Lee, Charlotte, and Timothy Gura. *Oral Interpretation.* 8th ed. Dallas, TX: Houghton Mifflin, 1992.

Long, Beverly, and Mary Francis HopKins. *Performing Literature.* Englewood Cliffs, NJ: Prentice-Hall, 1982.

Novelly, Maria C. *Theatre Games for Young Performers.* Colorado Springs, CO: Meriwether Publishing, Ltd., 1985.

Pelias, Ronald. *Performance Studies.* New York: St. Martin's Press, 1992.

Ratliffe, Gerald Lee. *Beginning Reader's Theatre: A Primer for Classroom Performance.* Urbana, IL: ERIC and Speech Communication Association, 1981.

Scher, A., and C. Verral. *100+ Ideas for Drama.* London: Heinemann Educational Books, 1978.

Temple, Charles, and Patrick Collins, eds. *Stories and Readers: New Perspectives on Literature in the Elementary Classroom.* Norwood, MA: Christopher-Gordon Publishers, 1992.

Valentine, Kristen, and Eugene Valentine. *Interlocking Pieces.* 3rd ed. Dubuque, IA: Kendall Hunt, 1991.

Yordon, Judy. *Roles in Interpretation.* 2d ed. Dubuque, IA: William C. Brown, 1989.

For reader's theatre scripts, write Theodore Kundrat, 400 E. Randolph Street #2208, Chicago, IL 60601.

## Nonprint Resources

Artana Productions, P.O. Box 1054, Marshfield, MA 02050.

Caedmon Records, Inc., 505 Eighth Ave., New York, NY 10018.

Design Video Communications, P.O. Box 30054, Indianapolis, IN 46230.

Gentle Wind, Songs and Stories for Children, Box 3103, Albany, NY 12203.

National Association for the Preservation and Perpetuation of Storytelling (NAPPS), P.O. Box 309, Jonesborough, TN 37659.

# NTC DEBATE AND SPEECH BOOKS

**Debate**

ADVANCED DEBATE, ed. Thomas & Hart
BASIC DEBATE, Fryar, Thomas, & Goodnight
COACHING AND DIRECTING FORENSICS, Klopf
CROSS-EXAMINATION IN DEBATE, Copeland
DICTIONARY OF DEBATE, Hanson
FORENSIC TOURNAMENTS: PLANNING AND ADMINISTRATION, Goodnight & Zarefsky
GETTING STARTED IN DEBATE, Goodnight
JUDGING ACADEMIC DEBATE, Ulrich
MODERN DEBATE CASE TECHNIQUES, Terry et al.
MOVING FROM POLICY TO VALUE DEBATE, Richards
STRATEGIC DEBATE, Wood & Goodnight
STUDENT CONGRESS & LINCOLN-DOUGLAS DEBATE, Giertz & Mezzera

**Speech Communication**

ACTIVITIES FOR EFFECTIVE COMMUNICATION, LiSacchi
THE BASICS OF SPEECH, Galvin, Cooper, & Gordon
CONTEMPORARY SPEECH, HopKins & Whitaker
CREATIVE SPEAKING, Buys et al.
DYNAMICS OF SPEECH, Myers & Herndon
GETTING STARTED IN PUBLIC SPEAKING, Prentice & Payne
LISTENING BY DOING, Galvin
LITERATURE ALIVE! Gamble & Gamble
MEETINGS: RULES & PROCEDURES, Pohl
PERSON TO PERSON, Galvin & Book
PUBLIC SPEAKING TODAY! Prentice & Payne
SELF-AWARENESS, Ratliffe & Herman
SPEAKING BY DOING, Buys, Sill, & Beck

 For a current catalog and information about our complete line of language arts books, write:
National Textbook Company,
a division of NTC Publishing Group
4255 West Touhy Avenue
Lincolnwood (Chicago), Illinois 60646-1975 U.S.A.